Fully for Life

Fully for Life

Expanding the Pro-Life Agenda

STEVEN R. TIMMERMANS

WIPF & STOCK · Eugene, Oregon

FULLY FOR LIFE
Expanding the Pro-Life Agenda

Copyright © 2024 Steven R. Timmermans. All rights reserved. Except for brief quotations in critical publications or reviews, no part of this book may be reproduced in any manner without prior written permission from the publisher. Write: Permissions, Wipf and Stock Publishers, 199 W. 8th Ave., Suite 3, Eugene, OR 97401.

Wipf & Stock
An Imprint of Wipf and Stock Publishers
199 W. 8th Ave., Suite 3
Eugene, OR 97401

www.wipfandstock.com

PAPERBACK ISBN: 979-8-3852-3024-2
HARDCOVER ISBN: 979-8-3852-3025-9
EBOOK ISBN: 979-8-3852-3026-6

Scriptures taken from the Holy Bible, New International Version®, NIV®. Copyright © 1973, 1978, 1984, 2011 by Biblica, Inc.™ Used by permission of Zondervan. All rights reserved worldwide. www.zondervan.com The "NIV" and "New International Version" are trademarks registered in the United States Patent and Trademark Office by Biblica, Inc.™

Dedication

This book is dedicated to our grandchildren who exemplify flourishing and overflowing lives through their words, energy, joy, and hugs. My prayer is that they will always cherish not just their Creator and their own lives, but the lives of all, nearby and far away, not yet born and those facing life each day: Aser Lankah, Bemnet Lankah, Ella Timmermans, Betselot Lankah, Saba Teshome, Miles Brower, Alleluia Lankah, Faben Teshome, and Kenna Timmermans.

Contents

Acknowledgments ix
Introduction xi

1. Initial Considerations for Approaching the Topic 1
2. Abortion and the Beginning of Life 11
3. Poverty: Living without Enough 25
4. Health and Wellness for Living 36
5. Disability: Lives Not to Be Overlooked 48
6. Seeking Life in a Culture of Gun Violence 60
7. Racism: A Sin That Diminishes Life 70
8. Incarceration and Criminal Justice: Life Locked Up 85
9. Welcoming the Sojourner: Living with Open Hearts 93
10. The Struggle for Life in War Zones 104
11. Promoting Life in a Post-Christian Era 116

Bibliography 121

Acknowledgments

I'M GRATEFUL THAT, AS before, the First CRC's men's book/spiritual accountability group read the manuscript, encouraged me as I tried to stay one or two chapters ahead of them, and provided me invaluable advice ranging from general encouragement to specific additions and clarifications. Thanks, as well, to fellow church member LaVerne Blickley and my wife, Barb Timmermans, for tackling specific chapters and providing reaction and suggestions. Finally, I'm grateful that throughout my life I've been part of communities whose faithful and thoughtful members have shaped my approach to all of life!

Introduction

I WAS IN HIGH school when the Supreme Court handed down its Roe v. Wade decision. While I can't pin down the exact moment or place where I became a pro-lifer, looking back it was pretty clear then that as a follower of Jesus, it was time to push back. I never picketed at Planned Parenthood, but I recall writing letters, obtaining bumper stickers (that my parents wouldn't let me put on the family car), and watching films of life in utero. Yet throughout those high school years, I don't recall Christian brothers and sisters bringing up two related issues, one specific to abortion and the other broader than abortion. No one asked, "When does life begin?" And no one questioned what else should be concerning to those advocating for life.

This book looks both at the classic pro-life issue of abortion as well as many other areas where the sanctity of life is threatened. The second chapter is unlike the others, for my purpose in this chapter is to encourage you to address the *a priori* question of when life begins—a question crucial to the abortion debate. The remaining chapters simply introduce areas where life is threatened for a part of humankind.

While my pro-life journey began in high school, it has broadened over the years. In many cases, life-events placed issues—in the form of real people—in my path. As I point out, by God's word and greater revelation, my pro-life agenda began to stretch in faithful ways. But I have remained perplexed why some—especially believers—have kept the agenda focused on only one item—abortion.

Introduction

In 1987, Ron Sider came out with his book *Completely Pro-Life*.[1] The subtitle, *Building a Consistent Stance on Abortion, The Family, Nuclear Weapons, The Poor* indicates the span he considered important then and when it was republished in 2010. But unfortunately, we still suffer from Christians being single issue believers and voters.

Many times I feel like an onlooker at a giant sporting event. The home team is well-funded, loud, and going on a rampage! Their number of wins is impressive and they show up on the evening news and in op-ed pieces. Yet I find myself confused. Do I really see myself as part of the home team and their single-mindedness? Are we really in a battle? Is there no good among those on the opposing team?

Indeed, I often want to distance myself from the home team which, for me, is the evangelical church. In recent years, I have been appalled at the thirst for cultural power and the chanting of "Make America Great Again." Jesus' words echo in my mind: "My kingdom is not of this world." The desire to mandate Christianity in government policies and laws is illusionary, for legalism doesn't save believers nor does it bring faith to unbelievers.

Back when I was the leader of a denomination, the challenges to full gospel living were bruising. Via emails, letters, and phone calls, the message was simple: Rise up against abortion, and ignore the rest of these "social gospel" issues. Of course, the messages were couched in more barely acceptable ways. "Lighten up on these other issues—the church isn't ready for them." "Don't you realize that the farmers aren't interested?" And "Look what happened to mainline Christianity."

Stretching my metaphor, sometimes I simply want to leave the arena and the game of church. For our calling isn't about taking sides—joining neither the home team nor the opposing team. Rather, I'd suggest we root for life in all of its many complexities. For life is precious, far more precious than political theater or competitive drama.

---

1. Sider, *Completely Pro-Life*.

INTRODUCTION

We need to step outside of the arena of church and hit the streets, valuing each life we encounter and sharing the source of all life wherever we can. Maybe, too, we'll encounter other Christ-followers in the boardrooms and homeless shelters of this world. There we will link hands together and live out the call for life. And maybe, just maybe, in being salt and light to the world, we'll help the North American evangelical church back to the ways of Christ and the cherishing of the crown of God's creation.

So, as you read the following chapters that focus on the sanctity of life in a variety of areas, ask yourself, Who are the proponents of life—do you know any? Do they sit in the pew next to you? Across the aisle from you? Further, each chapter ends with a question: What can you do to promote life? Because it's a question, I'm trying to point to some areas of possible focus, not complete answers. I trust the Spirit will lead.

1

Initial Considerations for Approaching the Topic

EACH OF US HAS a choice as we cruise through contemporary life in the Western world, discussing issues around the water cooler, seated at the dinner table, or after a worship service. On one hand, we can fall back on patterns that are comfortable and reassuring—much like cruising on auto-pilot. I hear phrases such as "I've always been a Republican," "I'm socially responsible," "I don't pay attention to politics." Falling back means resting upon what allows one to go forward on auto-pilot without careful thinking or in-depth analysis. Sometimes we do so on account of all the information we're bombarded with daily; it feels safe and secure to turn on the auto-pilot. However, we need to approach ideas and issues by postponing judgment, listening well, and digging deep for what is true, accurate, or reasonable.

I trust if you're reading this book, you have a faith commitment—a faith commitment that is shaped by the Judeo-Christian tradition, a faith commitment that provides a moral compass, a faith commitment that believes there are absolutes and all is not relative, a faith commitment that insists on valuing human life.

At times, with a faith commitment, it's easy to reach immediate conclusions: taking a life is wrong, adultery is wrong, stealing is wrong. Such conclusions can be traced back to the Ten Commandments—in other words, the Judeo-Christian tradition. Yet, a faith commitment shouldn't lead us to continually cruise on auto-pilot, as so much of life is colored in shades of grey, not simply black or white. Moreover, we have the words of Jesus in Matt 7:1–2:

> Do not judge, or you too will be judged. For in the same way you judge others, you will be judged, and with the measure you use, it will be measured to you.

Then Jesus suggests instead of judging the other, we examine ourselves in verses 3–5.

> Why do you look at the speck of sawdust in your brother's eye and pay no attention to the plank in your own eye? How can you say to your brother, "Let me take the speck out of your eye," when all the time there is a plank in your own eye? You hypocrite, first take the plank out of your own eye, and then you will see clearly to remove the speck from your brother's eye.

Yes, we who believe in Jesus might be too quick to judge, too quick to respond with certainty when considering others or their ideas, too complacent to switch off the auto-pilot. "I've always rejected pacifism as over-the-top Christianity, and therefore my mind is clear about war." "I've always found certain Christians too legalistic about Sunday observance, so I've learned that Sunday is a day to enjoy without adhering to specific rules." It's time to examine ourselves.

My concern is that simplistic and judgmental wading through life's tough issues can be incredibly problematic. Agreed, it's a habit that's hard to break . . . until something difficult enters your life. When your son tells you he's divorcing his wife, will you batten down the hatches, reach for some proof texts, and close your mind—and even your love—toward your son? Or will you set aside the habit, read some biblically based works on both sides of the issue, and listen? When your Muslim neighbor is seemingly noncommittal about 9/11, will you take your Bible, wave it in his face, and tell him he is headed for the same judgment those terrorists certainly received?

Initial Considerations for Approaching the Topic

To whom will you listen? What are faithful sources? How will you evaluate what you hear? Let me suggest a differentiation that arose out of the church's centuries-old struggles with asking such questions and sources for finding answers. The Belgic Confession, in addressing how we are to know God, says this:

> We know Him by two means: First, by the creation, preservation, and government of the universe; which is before our eyes as a most elegant book, wherein all creatures, great and small, are as so many characters leading us to *see clearly the invisible things of God*, even *his everlasting power and divinity*, as the apostle Paul says in Romans 1:20. All which things are sufficient to convince men and leave them without excuse. Second, He makes Himself more clearly and fully known to us by His holy and divine Word, that is to say, as far as is necessary for us to know in this life, to His glory and our salvation.[1]

Many refer to the first as *general revelation* and the second as *specific revelation*. That which is revealed generally is that which can be observed by a general audience. Specific revelation comes via the Bible, God's word.

In this post-Christian society, we will often fail at convincing others of the rightness or wrongness of something by appealing to God's word. For if someone fails to believe in God, he or she certainly doesn't find the Bible to be authoritative and convincing.

But general revelation is for a general audience, and if you and I believe God is the creator and author of this universe, this "most elegant book" will certainly not contradict Scripture while providing the common ground by which we all should be able to come to the truth.

Environmentalists may view a glorious sunset with appreciation without searching for the Creator of the universe. Physicians may observe the regenerative process in the human body but never consider the Designer. New parents may revel in the amazing progression of development in their little one, yet never step back to consider the Source. Moreover, without recognizing God's

---

1. De Bres, *Belgic Confession*, art. 2.

hand in creation, all kinds of people step into careers that seek to find truth.

I went to graduate school in order to study how abilities and emotions lead to flourishing or failure. And there I learned about the ways in which we can, using a mixture of probability statistics and careful analysis, come to greater knowledge from God's general revelation. Let me give you an example.

The teacher is complaining that third-grader Sam is not achieving in school. Why? Observation leads to the hunch that Sam's attentional system is the cause. But before coming to that conclusion, we test that hypothesis by comparing Sam's performance on some tests to the performance of a whole bunch of others; the latter gives us a picture of what is typical or normal. We see that Sam's attention is quite different than the typical pattern—a level of difference that is seemingly greater than just a chance snapshot.

Do you see the process involved? Often called the scientific process, this approach is used throughout the world in a variety of disciplines, all to better understand the natural world—including us humans. Stated differently, it is a way to dig deep into what God has provided us by general revelation.

Let's continue with this example of Sam. Now that we know his attentional skills are significantly different than what is typical, the physician wants to use a new medication to help him improve. But for a variety of reasons, the physician is very cautious. The physician has the pharmacist create four segments of dosages, each three weeks long, as the table below indicates. Each segment has a daily medication that Sam will take. However, the medication is only in segment one, segment two, and segment four. In segment three the pharmacist—by the physician's orders—places a sugar pill that looks just like the medication.

Segment 1 Weeks 1–3	Segment 2 Weeks 4–5	Segment 3 Weeks 7–9	Segment 4 Weeks 10–12
New Medication	New Medication	Sugar Pill (Placebo)	New Medication

Initial Considerations for Approaching the Topic

Next, at the end of each three-week long segment the tests for attention are given. Look at what might happen. One outcome would be that Sam's performance is unchanged—at the end of all four segments—and is exactly like his original performance that has been shown to be quite different from what is typical. A second outcome would be that at the end of each segment Sam's performance is considerably better—all four segments. A third outcome is that his performance was better at the end of segments one, two, and four, but at the end of segment three, it was back to the problematic level.

So what's going on? In the first outcome, it appears that the medication (and the sugar pill) doesn't seem to have an effect, so no need for Sam to take this medication. In outcome two, we have what's called the placebo effect—that somehow the hope of change creates change even though the third segment was only a sugar pill. It seems that hope influenced the testing, leading to no conclusions about the effectiveness of the medication, so again, no need for Sam to take this medication. But in outcome three, we can conclude that the medication seems to work, for Sam's results were improved at the end of each three-week segment when he was taking the medication, but not so during the third segment when it was just a sugar pill masquerading as the medication.

Notice, the effectiveness of the medication has been revealed through this careful process. Praise God for enabling us to come to better understandings of and improvements for Sam by peering into general revelation via this process.

Next, let's go back to the COVID-19 pandemic. Public health scientists were quickly acting in two ways. First, they encouraged us to use face masks, because they had a hunch that the virus was spreading by aerosol particles from an infected person to those around them. Their belief was that a mask might keep the infected person from spreading these particles and a non-infected person might be kept healthy by not breathing in such particles. Was there a careful testing of their hypothesis before making the recommendation? Not really. Was it appropriate to follow their recommendations? Yes, really! You see, while there wasn't time to do careful tests to determine that face masks worked beyond a doubt, these public health scientists had hunches based on what they knew about viruses in general and some observations that led them to believe the face masks would help control the pandemic.

The second thing scientists were doing was identifying an effective vaccine to protect us against the virus. Finding the exact formulary and then establishing its effectiveness is a slow, painstaking task; each time these scientists had a hunch they had found the right formulary, they would have to test it in ways somewhat similar to our example of Sam—albeit they had to do it with hundreds of people and wait for the outcomes.

Unfortunately, we seem to be in an era when science and the processes scientists use are often doubted. When faithful followers of Jesus do so, their faithfulness falters. Let me explain.

First, they are failing to adhere to this "most elegant book," God's general revelation. Science is not the enemy of belief; rather, scientific processes are an important way we are able to understand God's revelation to us.

Second, they are failing to adhere to God's specific revelation, God's word. Loving neighbor as self is a principle we are called to live by. So, as was the case in the third decade of this century, many asserted their individual freedoms, refusing to don masks. So, that's loving self and the freedoms oneself possesses. But what about neighbor? Donning a mask could be a very tangible way of loving your neighbor. The same is true about getting vaccinated. It seems to me that choosing masks and vaccinations are the best way to love neighbor as oneself.

Scaling this up and focusing on vaccinations, we may have missed an opportunity for herd immunity, in part, because of this self-centeredness. Consider what the World Health Organization says about herd immunity:

> "Herd immunity," also known as "population immunity," is the indirect protection from an infectious disease that happens when a population is immune either through vaccination or immunity developed through previous infection. WHO supports achieving 'herd immunity'

Initial Considerations for Approaching the Topic

> through vaccination, not by allowing a disease to spread through any segment of the population, as this would result in unnecessary cases and deaths. Herd immunity against COVID-19 should be achieved by protecting people through vaccination, not by exposing them to the pathogen that causes the disease. To safely achieve herd immunity against COVID-19, a substantial proportion of a population would need to be vaccinated, lowering the overall amount of virus able to spread in the whole population. The percentage of people who need to be immune in order to achieve herd immunity varies with each disease. For example, herd immunity against measles requires about 95% of a population to be vaccinated. The remaining 5% will be protected by the fact that measles will not spread among those who are vaccinated. For polio, the threshold is about 80%. The proportion of the population that must be vaccinated against COVID-19 to begin inducing herd immunity is not known.[2]

Notice my words were "in part." There were many reasons why herd immunity was not attained. The ever-mutating virus is one reason, and Mandavilli provided this summation back in the summer of 2021:

> Now, more than half of adults in the United States have been inoculated with at least one dose of a vaccine. But daily vaccination rates are slipping, and there is widespread consensus among scientists and public health experts that the herd immunity threshold is not attainable—at least not in the foreseeable future, and perhaps not ever.[3]

If 90 percent of the population had become vaccinated, would herd immunity have been achieved? Possible, but not probable. But nonetheless, believers—embracing the results from that "most elegant book," general revelation, and desiring to love their neighbor—should have created a stampede to the vaccination clinics.

---

2. World Health Organization, "Coronavirus Disease," paras. 1–5.
3. Mandavilli, "Reaching Herd Immunity Is Unlikely," para. 2.

But there was no stampede among fellow Christ-followers. A distrust of science? The difficulty of living into areas of life that are grey? Indeed, the challenge is to live in accord with the absolutes provided by the Creator. But we must remember that sometimes we claim too easily what we think is an absolute without consulting both books of revelation. And so, as we begin looking at the full spectrum of pro-life issues, my approach will be to rely on general revelation as well as specific revelation. Forwarding the ideas and words of Gordon Spykman, Steve Bishop notes this about general revelation:

> For Spykman the creation order is "the permanent and normative setting for human life in the world. God created a cosmos, not a chaos—a fully cohesive, beautifully interconnected world order." It is because of this that the sciences, for Christians and non-Christians, are feasible: all study is firmly grounded in the ontic order of creation, with all its varied topics of inquiry.[4]

Moreover, the overarching approach of this book seeks to understand how we can best love our neighbor, regardless of the specific issue, so that we can promote the flourishing of life for all—all of whom have been created in God's image.

As such, loving your neighbor contextualizes the following chapters. My wife, Barb, and I have lived in a university community, impoverished areas of town, adjacent to the Navajo reservation, and in the suburbs of Chicago and Grand Rapids. Each of those locales have opened up our eyes to understanding who is our neighbor. Moreover, when we left each of these contexts, we didn't lose our sense of our neighbors there. We're still neighbors to university students—it's not unusual to find one or two living with us. We're still neighbors to those with less, and remain connected through ministries such as a summer camp focused on the need for racial reconciliation founded by Barb's dad more than fifty years ago. We're still neighbors to friends in the American southwest, finding the best way to remain connected is by means

---

4. Bishop, "Everything Matters," 4.

Initial Considerations for Approaching the Topic

of financial gifts. We're still neighbors to suburban friends—neighbors with whom we pray and share daily life. Moreover, while we've not lived overseas, we've learned through our own experience with the adoptions of Yaineababa, Getenet, and Fekadu from Ethiopia when they were older that we have neighbors on the African continent. Far away? Not with modern technology that allows us to be in contact at a moment's notice. In addition, these experiences lead us to be engaged with newly arriving refugees, lending a hand of help and of friendship.

Toward the end of 2023 a Congolese refugee family took up residence in our church's Refugee Welcome Home. The first few weeks were intense, but the resettlement agency takes the lead. But after that initial time, life falls into a familiar rhythm, and our interactions more ordinary. Two stories demonstrate the delight of living life among neighbors. One day I learned the DVD player had died, and given the important of learning English (ask international students how they learned English—many will tell you it was American television), I ran out and purchased a DVD player, and since I had my three grandkids with me—ages four, five, and six and all of African parents—together we went to the Congolese family's home. As my back was turned to the kids as I tried to hook up the DVD player, something was going on—a gifting of love. For when I emerged from the project, I saw my three grandkids at the table eating plates full of African food with my friend Mama Ariada beaming!

And it was Ariada who decided in the first few months that our families needed to get to know each other. So, not too long later, all sixteen of them came to our house and joined most of our family, with only seven of our twenty-three missing. It was pure joy. Stories of coming to America were exchanged, challenges in child-rearing discussed, and favorite football teams (can't call it soccer with our new neighbors) were identified. It was an incarnational moment as Christ dined with us, establishing our new neighborhood.

So as Mr. Rogers would say, "welcome to the neighborhood!" As you step into the following chapters, recognize each instance for which the sanctity of life is addressed as well as impacts on neighbors nearby and far away whom we should love as much as or more than we love ourselves. And remember, open in front of us should be both books of revelation. In these ways, we will appropriately embrace the absolutes God holds forth to us as well as remain faithful to the many ways God makes himself known to us, even when the immediate answers are unclear and life is colored in shades of grey.

2

Abortion and the Beginning of Life

WE NEVER WROTE AN obituary. We never received sympathy cards. We never held a funeral service.

We had two miscarriages in our younger years, and neither was accompanied with these familiar indicators of the passing of life. Why did we skip the obituaries, rarely receive a spoken word or written card of sympathy, and not observe the hope of resurrected life?

It makes me wonder: Does life begin at conception? Repeatedly we hear in the abortion debate that it does. This debate—about abortion and the beginning of life—has captivated the energies of believers ever since Roe v. Wade legalized abortion in the United States. Suddenly, pro-life became the rallying cry of congregations, ordinary folks began picketing Planned Parenthood, and a decades-long effort to reshape the Supreme Court began. Sermons pointed out the evil of abortion, billboards showed pictures of fetuses with symbolized heart beats, and Christian leaders suggested if we looked the other way, we'd be as guilty as the German church during the time of Hitler. The ironic thing is that it wasn't until much later after Roe v. Wade that Christian evangelical leaders began to aggressively fight against abortion. It is important, therefore, to review the mid-century history.

In partnership with *Christianity Today*, the Christian Medical Society met in 1968 to address issues related to reproduction and abortion. The conclusions coming from this meeting were much more varied and nuanced than what we hear today. For example, the twenty-five leaders said that "whether or not the performance of an induced abortion is sinful we are not agreed, but about the necessity and permissibility for it under certain circumstances we are in accord."[1] They concluded that "the Christian physician will advise induced abortion only to safeguard greater values sanctioned by Scripture. These values may be individual, familial, or societal."[2] The statement goes on, focusing on the justification of abortion when the life of the mother is at risk, in cases of rape or incest, or when the "continuation of the pregnancy is likely to result in the birth of a child with grave physical deformities or mental retardation."[3] Leah Scanzoni's 1973 book noted the Bible's silence on abortion, so, she relayed, some Christians believe, particularly in light of Exod 21:22–23, that "a developing embryo or fetus was not regarded as a full human being";[4] it is not insignificant that James Dobson, founder of Focus on the Family, provided an introduction for Scanzoni's book.

At the 1971 meeting of the Southern Baptist Convention (SBC), a resolution was passed calling for a legalization of abortion (reaffirmed in 1974 and 1976). Even more interesting is what a leader of the SBC said back then:

> When the Roe decision was handed down, W. A. Criswell, pastor of First Baptist Church in Dallas and sometime president of the Southern Baptist Convention, issued a statement praising the ruling. "I have always felt that it was only after a child was born and had a life separate from its mother that it became an individual person," Criswell declared, "and it has always, therefore, seemed to me that what is best for the mother and for the future should be allowed."[5]

1. *Christianity Today*, "Protestant Affirmation," para. 4.
2. *Christianity Today*, "Protestant Affirmation," para. 11.
3. *Christianity Today*, "Protestant Affirmation," para. 31.
4. Scanzoni, *Sex Is a Parent Affair*, 147.
5. Balmer, "Evangelical Abortion Myth," para. 5.

Abortion and the Beginning of Life

While it is tempting to explore the shift especially among Christian evangelicals, it is more important to focus on the current situation, particularly because in 2022, Roe v. Wade was overturned by the Supreme Court, ending abortion as a constitutional right and handing decision making to the states.[6] While for some this was the victory they were working for, the issue of abortion and being pro-life has not become any less conflictual in our society. Now we see some states chasing out abortion providers and those seeking abortions traveling to other states that still make abortion available. In some respects, this hodgepodge of public policies and laws makes the topic even more complex and challenging. The debate is far from over.

But as we face the complexity of laws and opinions, we should begin with a basic question: When does life begin? First, a review of the biology, then some perspectives found in society on the beginning of life and abortion, and finally some reflections on faithful discernment. While this discussion will rely heavily on general revelation, we should never lose sight of the sanctity of life—a foundational biblical truth.

BIOLOGICAL DEVELOPMENT

Gestation begins when sperm and egg come together to form a zygote. Pregnancy counting begins with the last menstrual period, so this fertilization happens at the beginning of the third week of a woman's four-week menstrual cycle. Fertilization occurs in the fallopian tubes—something to recall when we consider ectopic pregnancies in subsequent paragraphs.

The zygote has forty-six chromosomes with twenty-three from the mother and twenty-three from the father. In subsequent paragraphs we will also return to chromosomes as we consider chromosomal abnormalities.

---

6. Totenberg and McCammon, "Supreme Court Overturns Roe v. Wade," para. 1.

The zygote leaves the fallopian tubes and enters the uterus as the single cell begins to divide, forming a morula—a cluster of cells.

Then, at week four, the ball of cells continues to divide, is now called a blastocyst, and implants into the lining of the uterus. The inner cells of the blastocyst become the embryo and the outer cells, the placenta. As the development continues, the embryo develops into three layers, with the various layers giving rise to the nervous system, eyes, and inner ears; to the heart and circulatory system; and to the lungs and intestines.

At week six, the neural tube closes, giving rise to the development of the brain and spinal cord. The embryo takes on a C shape as other organs begin to develop as well. Then, at week ten, the embryo is called a fetus. During the remaining weeks of the first trimester, the development of additional organs begins.

The second trimester includes the beginning of eye movement (week sixteen), of hearing (week eighteen), and of thumb sucking (week twenty-one). It is during the middle of this trimester that the mother begins to feel movement of the fetus, and around week twenty-five, the fetus begins to recognize sounds such as the mother's voice.

The third trimester is a time of rapid growth as the fetus gains weight, the eyes open, and much movement occurs.

Notice, as you have read the preceding paragraphs, you could arrive at any number of conclusions, identifying any one of various points in fetal development as the time that you believe is the beginning of life. Or, you might even admit that biological development doesn't fully answer the question of when life begins.

ABORTION AND THE DEFINITION OF LIFE

With the United States' Supreme Court ending the nearly fifty years of legal abortion across America in 2022, the matter of allowing or banning abortion became the responsibility of each state. While some states maintained the mother's right to an abortion, many other states decided to restrict abortion with a great variety of definitions as to the beginning of life. Some states allowing abortion prohibit it after fetal viability—that, should birth occur, the child could survive, most often understood as twenty-one weeks gestation. Other states have taken legislative action to limit or end abortion but with variety in the possibility of exceptions or drastically restricting the cut-off time. And at the time of penning this chapter, one state has defined the beginning of life to be realized already with embryos—those frozen and not implanted in the uterus.[7] It is difficult, however, to describe completely the status of all fifty states, since many states are in transition with their laws.

Nevertheless, at this point in time, it appears a dozen states have outlawed abortion entirely, some with no exceptions and others with exceptions such as rape/incest, danger to the mother's life, and/or fetal abnormalities. Other states have drawn the line at six, twelve, or fifteen weeks.

Whether allowing abortion or significantly restricting it, states often have additional requirements such as counseling and, in the case of minors, parental notification or approval.

A related factor is the "morning after" pill that is taken within five days of unprotected sex. Some voices suggest if life begins at conception, this is a form of abortion; at the time of this writing, no states have outlawed these medications. However, other abortion drugs, available for use up to ten weeks, may become restricted. Wyoming has made it illegal to sell or prescribe such abortion drugs, and a federal judge in Texas has placed a temporary injunction on their use, although another federal judge in Washington has circumvented that ruling with an action ensuring the FDA continues to make this drug available in seventeen states.

DISCERNING THE BEGINNING OF LIFE

We need only to look at the abortion issue to understand the variety of definitions used to define the beginning of life. And so, if we look to legislative bodies and actions to outlaw, limit, or

---

7. Chandler, "Warnings of the Impact," para. 1.

allow abortion, we would find a variety of definitions: life begins at conception, at six weeks, at twelve weeks, at fifteen weeks, or twenty-one weeks! It seems that our Creator points us to general revelation but, instead of a clear answer, the task is discernment.

Consider the variety of views among the general public. The Pew Research Center has provided empirically assessed opinions of Americans on this question.

Nearly four-in-ten endorse the notion that "human life begins at conception, so a fetus is a person with rights (26% say this describes their views extremely well, 12% very well)."[8] This means, then, a bit more than 60 percent believe the beginning of life occurs sometime after conception, a view that we will explore soon.

But before continuing this search as to the beginning of life, the Pew Research Center also helps us understand views about abortion, beginning with white evangelical Christians: "nearly three-quarters say that abortion should be against the law in all cases without exception (21%) or that it should be illegal in most cases (53%)." A slim majority of Catholics (53 percent) also view abortion as morally wrong, but many also say it is morally acceptable in most (24 percent) or all cases (4 percent), or that it is not a moral issue (17 percent).[9]

This Pew report also finds that relatively few Americans view the morality of abortion in stark terms: Overall, just 7 percent of all US adults say abortion is morally acceptable in all cases, and 13 percent say it is morally wrong in all cases. A third say that abortion is morally wrong in *most* cases, while about a quarter (24 percent) say it is morally acceptable most of the time.[10]

While it appears 80 percent are somewhere in the middle by avoiding absolutism; the Pew report goes on to describe how a segment of the United States' population—particularly evangelical Christians—believe abortion is wrong in most or all cases. Does this relate to their belief that life begins at conception?[11]

    8. Pew, "America's Abortion Quandary," 57.
    9. Pew, "America's Abortion Quandary," 50.
    10. Pew, "America's Abortion Quandary," 50.
    11. Pew, "America's Abortion Quandary," 22.

In our review of human fetal development, one could draw the line at a number of different places to mark the beginning of life: at conception, at ten weeks when we begin to call the embryo a fetus, at the beginning of the second trimester, during the second trimester when the mother begins to feel movement, or up to the point of viability for birth—usually no sooner than twenty-one weeks.

While it is possible to understand the logic of all of these definitions, it is helpful to turn to those who address ethical and philosophical questions from the vantage point of faith. Henry Stob was one such individual, serving both at Calvin College (now Calvin University) and Calvin Theological Seminary for decades in the previous century, relying on general revelation and specific revelation.

Stob begins with this observation: "The fetus in an in-between entity. It is obviously not a simple ununited spermatozoon, nor a simple unfertilized ovum. It is also not a postpartum baby or infant. It exists somewhere between these things. That is why people have disputed about the exact nature or status, and about whether it can be destroyed without moral fault." He goes on to say this entity is "something in the process of becoming human."[12]

Stob then reviews answers given by science, philosophy, theology, and law. Remembering Stob's reflections are nearly fifty years past, he notes that science sees in conception that the fetal tissue contains a complete genetic package—something which is the core of humanness. But then, still utilizing a scientific perspective, he notes that the fertilized egg doesn't become an embryo until it is implanted in the uterus and, if implantation doesn't occur, fertilized eggs are lost in the menstrual stream.

It seems that an important question is this: Might it be that the fertilized egg is only a blueprint for life until implantation occurs? With this focus, might a more legitimate definition of the beginning of life be "upon implantation," and not "at conception"?

Stob provides a rich history in attempting to bring light to this subject. He recalls that the Stoics thought the fetus in utero

12. Stob, *Ethical Reflections*, 229–30.

was thought of as part of the mother—merely, says Stob, *spes animantes*, not *homo*, nor *infans*. He uses the example of fruit—that it is understood as part of the tree until it falls. He also recounts the positions of Augustine and Thomas Aquinas. These ancient philosophers believed that the body was created before the soul, and so the embryo was not a human until it had a soul. However, although Augustine made differentiation based on the soul—*embryo informatus* (before having a soul) and *embryo formatus* (upon having a soul)—he did not define when this differentiation occurred. Some during that period, however, identified the change occurring at the point the mother first feels movement. Finally, Stob consults fifteenth-century English law, finding it defined the beginning of life at the moment of quickening—when the mother first feels movement.

After these reviews, Stob makes a conclusion about the genesis of life before addressing the issue of abortion directly: "Because of what I have called the in-between status of the fetus I do not regard its destruction as tantamount to infanticide. What is destroyed in abortion is not a human being; at most it is something in process of becoming human. This, of course, is a great deal; and the fetus therefore deserves everyone's respect and protection. But one is not entitled to speak too quickly and too loudly of murder when the question of abortion is raised, particularly when it concerns the embryo in the very earliest stages of its existence."[13]

Stob provides us insight by using the phrase "something in the process of becoming human." Do we go back to the earlier definitions of philosophers and theologians? Do we define life at uterine implantation or with quickening? Do we live with the ambiguity of Augustine or even Stob's definition of "in-betweenness?"

Unfortunately, for those who call themselves Christian as well as those who don't, we live in a time where the general public is quick to ignore science. As mentioned previously, the public health debates about vaccines and face masks during the pandemic of the early 2020s showed that there is often, especially in some quarters, a mistrust of science. That being said, I doubt if a precise

13. Stob, *Ethical Reflections*, 232.

Abortion and the Beginning of Life

definition based on biology would be fully accepted by many in society; thus, a definition such as uterine implantation could be easily cast aside. But at the other end of the continuum, quickening might be considered too subjective in our current society.

I would hope that Christians would embrace this notion of in-between and, from it, closely examine where they fall on the continuum of the beginning of life. I would hope, too, that Christians of varying communions could each arrive at their own definitions. Historically, Catholics have constructed a different paradigm, not looking at the destruction of an embryo or fetus, but instead focusing on the wasting of the spermatozoa—thereby declaring even *coitus interruptus* a sin. Protestants have much greater differences in understanding, but I would urge its various communions to seek definitions of the beginning of life while holding on to this notion of in-betweenness. Some might rely on quickening or, as is often the case in the medical field and even state law, fetal viability (usually related to twenty-one weeks gestation). Others might adopt positions much earlier in gestational development, all the way to the implantation of the fertilized egg to the uterine wall. For when we define life, then we can begin to address the issue of abortion.

Notice my call is to Christian communions, not to society and its lawmakers, judges, and citizens. It may be the case in the United States that we will live with a variety of abortion laws specific to each state for quite some time, or a federal law could come into play instituting a single standard. But in my call to Christian communions, I believe the first order of business is at once both personal and communal: there is a significant need for communities of belief to define the beginning of life and then live with that definition.

What might be the result? Might those of the Roman Catholic communion continue in their historical positions? Might other Protestants define the beginning of life as viability and still others implantation? Is it even possible for various Christian communions to have differences of opinion—relying on either specific revelation or general revelation?

We must have civil discourse within the faith community, for while God's word is absolute in prohibiting the taking of life, what we know from general revelation is that there are multiple points at which the beginning of life can be claimed. But in addition to defining the beginning of life, there are multiple opinions about exceptions—far more, seemingly, than fifty years ago. So, first we return to the Pew report:

> While about half of White evangelical Protestants (51%) say abortion should be legal if a pregnancy threatens the woman's life or health, clear majorities of other Protestant groups and Catholics say this should not be the case. The same pattern holds in views of whether abortion should be legal if the pregnancy is the result of rape. Most White non-evangelical Protestants (75%), Black Protestants (71%) and Catholics (66%) say abortion should be permitted in this instance, while White evangelicals are more divided: 40% say it should be legal, while 34% say it should be illegal and about a quarter say it depends. Mirroring the pattern seen among adults overall, opinions are more varied about a situation where a baby might be born with severe disabilities or health issues. For instance, half of Catholics say abortion should be legal in such cases, while 21% say it should be illegal and 27% say it depends on the situation. Most religiously unaffiliated adults—including overwhelming majorities of self-described atheists—say abortion should be legal in each of the three circumstances.[14]

Let's focus just on the first one: when the life of the mother is at risk. While this could take on a number of situations, let's focus on just one: ectopic pregnancies—where the fertilized egg implants in the fallopian tube instead of the uterine wall. Not only will the fertilized egg not survive, but it brings grave danger to the mother. The solution, if caught early enough, is to administer a drug to stop the cells from growing, thereby ending the pregnancy. Surgery is the second route and could result in removal of the entire fallopian tube.

---

14. Pew, "America's Abortion Quandary," 43.

Abortion and the Beginning of Life

Notice, with both solutions, a pregnancy is terminated. Some might label it abortion. So, importantly, when does life begin? Unless you define conception as the beginning of life, many would consider this a just and right decision. Moreover, even if you define conception as the beginning of life, you may be able to endorse this due to the fact that it puts the mother's life in danger.

Consider US Senator Rand Paul. In the past, he introduced Senate Bill 583, entitled the Life at Conception Act, yet Paul mentioned thousands of exceptions; his chief of staff provided this clarification: "By 'thousands of exceptions,' Stafford told LifeSiteNews.com, Paul meant that a singular exception to save the life of the mother would likely cover thousands of individual cases—for example, ectopic pregnancies or others that directly threaten the mother's life. Stafford did not address Senator's position on abortions in the case of rape or incest in the interview."[15]

By now I trust you find this topic quite muddled, both in terms of the defining when life begins and exceptions. My challenge to the reader remains: Within your faith communion, identify your stance on the beginning of life, whether abortion can be tolerated before that point in time (unless, of course, you define the beginning of life as conception), and whether there are any possible exceptions.

Admittedly, this is not a solution many will like. We long for a clear, biblically based definition for the beginning of life (which some believe is the case). We look to government for such rules, or more often, expect the government to hold the rules we believe. Moreover, in some communions, my suggestion to follow the church's lead is often ignored. Then, too, when we look at what other communions believe, we may recoil into self-righteousness. Why is it, for example, that nearly three-fourths of black Protestants believe abortion is allowable if the life or health of the mother is at risk—is there something in the history of black Americans that cherishes the life of mothers?

Remember that whether we continue to have a patchwork of state legislation or someday have a federal definition, you may

---

15. Abad-Santos, "Paul Rand Isn't 100% Pro-Life," para. 1.

have to live at odds with society's pronouncement. Amid a plurality among believers and legislation you may or may not believe is just, simply hold to your position, use your voice to encourage a solution you believe is faithful, and show mercy and compassion to those around you who hold other positions.

FOCUSING ON THE GOAL

So, then, what does it mean to be pro-life? Remember, a fellow believer from a communion different from yours or even the person next to you in the pew may be pro-life yet embrace a position that may differ from yours based on the definition of the beginning of life or understanding the role of exceptions. Rather than squabbling about various positions that can be legitimately embraced based on careful thinking and understandings, focus on the goal: life.

And if you focus on life, children who otherwise might have been aborted (theoretically all children!) require us to be pro-life in the long haul. It's not enough to advocate for birth when a pregnancy is unwanted; we must also advocate for life. Think about it as pro-life for all of life, or, in short, life-long pro-life.

Have you thought about the great number of fertilized eggs achieved through in vitro fertilization (IVF) that will not be implanted? (Clearly, the courts in Alabama have!) Even before we consider test tube conception, please be reminded that "between one-third and one-half of all fertilized eggs [achieved via intercourse] never fully implant."[16] Some have taken note, however, that fertilized eggs achieved via IVF still have the opportunity for life via adoption implantation, unlike those fertilized via intercourse but not implanted. As Mallenbaum notes, "'Embryo adoption' is the term a number of embryo donor services primarily in Christian circles use to describe transferring the extra frozen embryo cells of an IVF patient to an individual or couple. It's a term typically preferred by faith-based organizations that specialize in embryo

16. Gold, "Implications of Defining," para. 6.

Abortion and the Beginning of Life

donation and emphasize the prevention of those frozen cells from being discarded or used in research."[17] Especially for Christians who believe life begins at conception, this is another way to be pro-life. Or, as Henry Stob might say, this is still another form of in-betweenness—and embryo adoption brings about ultimate human fruition. Of course, Christians (as well as others) who do not believe life begins at conception have less concern about discarding these frozen embryos, possibly not unlike eggs fertilized via intercourse that are not implanted.

It is also necessary to consider being pro-life once babies are born. For example, consider the number of children in foster care. "In 2021, 203,770 children under 18 entered foster care in the United States, a rate of 3 per 1,000. The rate of entry has hovered at 3 or 4 per 1,000 for two decades. Kids ages 1 to 5 make up the largest share (29% in 2021) of children entering care. National data also show that Black and American Indian and Alaska Native children continue to be overrepresented among those entering foster care."[18] This report goes on to remind us that these children entering the foster care system are often neglected or abused and carry trauma that may interfere with development down the road. In light of these statistics and needs, what does it mean to be life-long pro-life? Becoming foster parents? Adopting foster children? Supporting those who do either or both? What do we hear from our pulpits? See in our Sunday School classrooms?

The number of things we must consider to be life-long pro-life advocates for children is great. While a pro-life lobby may focus on the issue of abortion, our communities should seek the sanctity of life for all of our children.

But now, back to our miscarriages. I don't think our extended family and friends nor our church messed up. In neither case were we close to fetal viability; moreover, in the second case, a chorionic villi sampling showed the fetus to be disabled in a way that was incompatible with life. It is probably clear that neither we nor our

---

17. Mallenbaum, "Embryo 'Adoption,'" para 3.

18. Annie E. Casey Foundation, "Child Welfare and Foster Care Statistics," para. 8.

church communion then believed that life begins at conception. I might add, however, that for those who believe life begins at conception, they have a tremendous task in turning their beliefs into ministry practice when it comes to miscarriages.

Alternatively, let me end with a sad but beautiful story of connecting beliefs about the beginning of life to practice. Our oldest daughter and her husband miscarried at twenty weeks—nearly the point of viability. They named their daughter Mabel, the chaplain performed baptism and attended to our loss, and together we grieved as family members and with their church as this child's few moments of life ended in death.

WHAT YOU CAN DO TO PROMOTE LIFE

Life is a gift. Created in God's image, our responsibilities to the unborn and the born involve discernment and require faithfulness. If you are in a conversation about abortion, one of the best questions you can ask is "When does life begin?" Helping your brother or sister tie this basic belief to the issue of abortion brings clarity. While you might be eager to debase them of their belief that life begins at viability, at fifteen weeks, or at conception, better to ask why they believe so.

We must allow believers to have differences of opinion and resist the temptation to impose our own particular view on all. And if that's not complicated enough, we need to be both gracious and truth-tellers in a pluralistic society with ever changing public policies and laws.

3

Poverty: Living without Enough

A GREAT NUMBER OF years ago, we opened our home to a high schooler in our neighborhood. The immediate cause was that a bunch of relatives were coming, and he knew he'd be displaced to some corner of his house. He was the youngest of four being raised by a single parent who never held a job, moved about every year, and had difficulties succeeding. In short, poverty was nipping at her heels with every step she took.

Once this young man moved in, we learned more about his life. He talked about taking food and hiding it, so that when he was hungry, he could be assured he'd have something to eat. Things were so different in our home, just a few blocks over, that he wrote an essay about life with us for his high school composition class. The topic was dinner time—that you could plan on it every day at 5:30!

POVERTY

Lacking the basic financial resources so that each day is a challenge—a challenge to satiate hunger, a challenge to ensure a roof over your head, a challenge to keep growing kids clothed. Certainly, these things are basic needs of life, and poverty interferes.

FIGURE 1

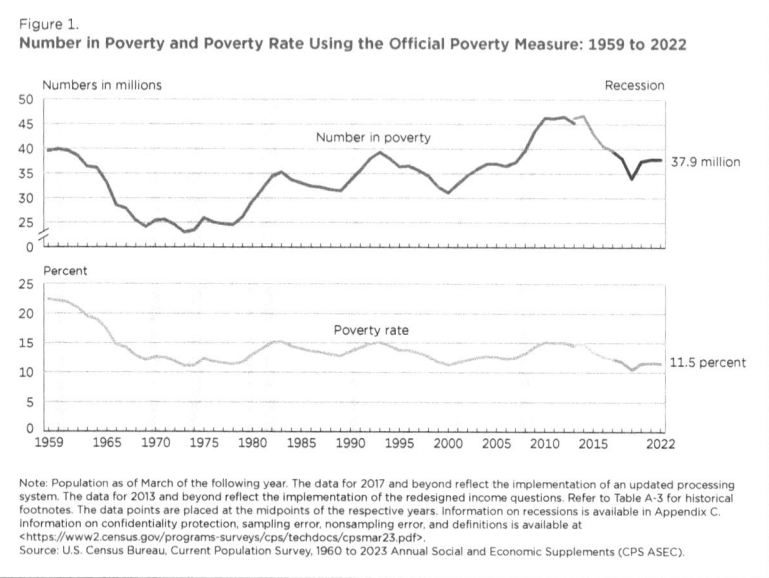

This chart from the U.S. Census Bureau shows the numbers and percentages of those in poverty the last sixty-three years.[1] The last year of the graph and that which is available shows almost thirty-eight million Americans—more than one person in every ten—is in poverty. These data use the federal definition of poverty: "the Census Bureau uses a set of money income thresholds that vary by family size and composition to determine who is in poverty. If a family's total income is less than the family's threshold, then that family and every individual in it is considered in poverty."[2] For example, in 2023, an individual with an income under $14,580 was considered in poverty; a family of four with an income under $30,000 was considered in poverty. However, many programs serve those whose income falls below 150 percent of the poverty level, so in the example above, if income was below $45,000, the family might be eligible for some assistance. Moreover, this connects to

1. United States Census Bureau, "National Poverty in America," Figure 1.
2. United States Census Bureau, "How the Census Bureau Measures," para. 1.

Poverty: Living without Enough

the issue of the working poor. The United Way uses the acronym ALICE: Asset Limited, Income Constrained, Employed.[3]

As you might expect, poverty varies by ethnicity and geography. The percentage of 11.5 was across all people. But, the U.S. Census Bureau has found that the rate for black people was 17.1 percent compared to 8.6 percent for whites; for non-white Hispanics, the rate is more than double whites as well. Interestingly, the poverty rates for non-metro (i.e., rural) Blacks, American Indians, and Alaskan natives is higher than those in urban areas. When relying on the ALICE definition, the authors note that this status "spans all races, ages, ethnicities, and abilities, though households of color are disproportionately ALICE."[4]

The statistics could fill page after page, but most importantly, poverty is a threat to life. Poor nutrition, health challenges, uneven educational attendance, and unemployment all result in immediate or long-term suffering. The challenges pile up. Poor nutrition may mean compromised learning in school. Health challenges may keep an otherwise employable person out of the job market. Unemployment may result in some assistance, but often not enough to get out of poverty.

Award-winning author Matthew Desmond's book *Poverty, By America* looks at why the United States has more poverty than any other "advanced democracy." He looks at three areas: exploitation, a lopsided welfare state, and segregation and bifurcation.

He examines *exploitation*, looking at things that hinder a competitive labor market (using contracted workers over employing them, rules against unionizing, etc.) and affordable housing (rising costs of rent, lack of mortgage access, and the like). He turns our attention to banks—banks that often avoid opening branches in poorer neighborhoods, thereby opening the door to ruthless lenders. Back to traditional banking, he reports that 9 percent of those holding accounts with average balances of $350 or less pay 84 percent of overdraft fees.[5] Rather than believing that

---

3. United Way, "About Us: Meet ALICE," para. 1.
4. United Way, "About Us: Meet ALICE," para. 2.
5. Desmond, *Poverty, By America*, 71.

the financial sector has forgotten the poor, he suggests that this sector willfully exploits the poor.

As I've walked beside refugees new to America, they are sitting ducks for such exploitation. For one family, an emergency room visit within the first four weeks of their arrival triggered a bill that they missed, and within a couple of months, the hospital had shifted their account to a collection agency. Why had this happened? It's difficult to ascertain, but about the third week after arrival is the switch from "general Medicaid" to one's specific Medicaid plan that covers a refugee in Michigan. That was the time of the ER visit. By the time the resettlement agency righted the error, I can only suspect that their credit score, in its infancy, tanked—which will be problematic for a host of financial steps coming ahead.

Desmond concludes we have a *lopsided welfare state* as he examines who uses aid. Those who need it the most, he reports, do not access the benefits of food stamps, government health insurance, unemployment insurance (for those between jobs), and Supplemental Security—a value of nearly $142 billion each year. In contrast, wealthier Americans seize opportunities such as tax breaks on employer health insurance, mortgage interest deductions, and 529 plans.[6] Why might this be? Accessing benefits often requires skill with online submissions, experience with legal matters, and personal financial records from a month ago to years past. You can guess which side of the divide is better suited for governmental applications.

Might Desmond's conclusion be true? Back to the story of the young man who moved in with us during his high school years. When it was time to go to college, we asked his mom about records of taxes she had filed. She had never filed a tax return! In retrospect, when one doesn't earn any income, there's little reason to file. Nevertheless, in order to afford college, this young man needed to get as much financial aid as possible. So, we—the affluent ones—coached him and his mother through the processes, making sure he could take advantage of all the financial aid he was

---

6. Desmond, *Poverty, By America*, 89–90, 93.

POVERTY: LIVING WITHOUT ENOUGH

due. If we hadn't assisted in this way, I suspect all of that aid might have been missed, and he might have missed the opportunity for getting his bachelors degree (and two masters degrees after that!).

Segregation and bifurcation, according to Desmond, leads to the concentration of wealth in exclusive communities. From zoning laws to the benefits of pricey neighborhoods—good schools, safety, etc.—all serve to bifurcate American society into two different groups.

Our youngest child, Fekadu, came into our family from an orphanage in Ethiopia at the age of eleven. Our other children were in a private Christian school, and so that's where Fekadu started his schooling in America as well. However, he had no English, and the school had no English as a Second Language program. Yet, it was a great school with great teachers; plus we privately hired an in-school tutor to ensure he was making the grade: the benefit of affluence.

I often compare suburban, private schooling for Fekadu with what a recent refugee I work with is experiencing. Enock is nine and in a caring, cosmopolitan city public school. Yet, as the first few months demonstrated, school wasn't working for him. Soon the teacher was contacting us about bad behavior.

Thankfully, we went to work, trying to compensate for the typical bifurcated educational story. For Enock, we created a plan to incentivize good behavior (when a youngster doesn't understand most everything, behavior can turn south) which worked out beautifully. More importantly, with tutors from our church, he has been making amazing progress in math. Even math requires English, and the names of numbers were initially well beyond him, and while he has not caught up to the class's focus on multiplication, we are doing two column addition with carrying—an amazing thing in just three short months.

Read Desmond's book to find out the ways in which he thinks we can address poverty, changing the structures and systems that keep people impoverished. While the stories about Fekadu and Enock help us remember the causes Desmond cites, they are stories about addressing individuals, not the inequity in the educational system. If we are to promote the flourishing of life for all, we need to focus on systems, not just our neighbors.

For example, we can learn much from a recent history of governmental funding and tax credits triggered by the pandemic and then discontinued. A study from the Brookings Institution provides this report:

> The 2021 expansion of the Child Tax Credit (CTC) led to a historic reduction in poverty in the United States, particularly for children. Research showed that child poverty fell immediately and substantially. The Census's Supplemental Poverty Measure (SPM) showed that children from all racial and ethnic minority groups experienced relatively large reductions in poverty rates, but that SPM poverty rates fell most dramatically for Black and Hispanic children. Black child poverty rates fell by 17 percentage points between 2009 and 2021, while SPM child poverty rates fell from 30% to 8% among Hispanic children over the same period.[7]

Amazing pro-life results! "Parents primarily reported using the child tax credit dollars on things like basic household necessities, rent, childcare, school supplies, groceries."[8] However, as the one-year expansion of tax credits expired, childhood poverty shot up—to 12.4 percent in 2022 from the 2021 low of 5.2 percent and beyond the pre-pandemic level of 9.7 percent.[9]

Finally, in 2024 Congress partially extended this credit seeing how it made such a significant impact. Was the pro-life lobby engaged in the debate, pointing out how important this extension would be to the sanctity of life?

Other examples of government attempts to address poverty include food stamps, welfare, unemployment, and other such programs most often provided at the state level. Some consider these a problem. Back in 1976 while campaigning, Ronald Reagan often mentioned a woman he named the Welfare Queen, accusing her of

---

7. Hardy et al., "Anti-Poverty Effects," 1.
8. Sy and Cuevas, "Child Poverty Increases Sharply," para. 1.
9. Sy and Cuevas, "Child Poverty Increases Sharply," paras. 4–5.

ripping off the government by taking aid she wasn't entitled to. She was not a fabrication, and her deceit and abuse of the system was real, extensive, and shocking.[10] But should we conclude assistance is bad just because of one woman?

According to Schnurer, the fraud so many believe is epidemic in the system is not necessarily true:

> It's not easy to get agreement on actual fraud levels in government programs. Unsurprisingly, liberals say they're low, while conservatives insist they're astronomically high. In truth, it varies from program to program. One government report says fraud accounts for less than 2 percent of unemployment insurance payments. It's seemingly impossible to find statistics on "welfare" (i.e., TANF) fraud, but the best guess is that it's about the same. A bevy of inspector general reports found "improper payment" levels of 20 to 40 percent in state TANF programs—but when you look at the reports, the payments appear all to be due to bureaucratic incompetence (categorized by the inspector general as either "eligibility and payment calculation errors" or "documentation errors"), rather than intentional fraud by beneficiaries.[11]

Another belief differs from concerns about fraud. Instead, the concern is that people become dependent on governance assistance and do not take responsibility for their own situation (pulling themselves up by their own bootstraps), and also spend the money on non-essentials. Politicians often hitch their campaigns to such thinking. Consider the legacy of Ronald Reagan's time in office.

> By the end of Reagan's term in office federal assistance to local governments was cut 60 percent. Reagan eliminated general revenue sharing to cities, slashed funding for public service jobs and job training, almost dismantled federally funded legal services for the poor, cut the anti-poverty Community Development Block Grant program

10. Demby, "Truth behind the Lies."
11. Schnurer, "Just How Wrong," para. 4.

and reduced funds for public transit. The only "urban" program that survived the cuts was federal aid for highways—which primarily benefited suburbs, not cities. These cutbacks had a disastrous effect on cities with high levels of poverty and limited property tax bases, many of which depended on federal aid. In 1980 federal dollars accounted for 22 percent of big city budgets. By the end of Reagan's second term, federal aid was only 6 percent. The most dramatic cut in domestic spending during the Reagan years was for low-income housing subsidies. Reagan appointed a housing task force dominated by politically connected developers, landlords and bankers. In 1982 the task force released a report that called for "free and deregulated" markets as an alternative to government assistance—advice Reagan followed. In his first year in office Reagan halved the budget for public housing and Section 8 to about $17.5 billion. And for the next few years he sought to eliminate federal housing assistance to the poor altogether. In the 1980s the proportion of the eligible poor who received federal housing subsidies declined. In 1970 there were 300,000 more low-cost rental units (6.5 million) than low-income renter households (6.2 million). By 1985 the number of low-cost units had fallen to 5.6 million, and the number of low-income renter households had grown to 8.9 million, a disparity of 3.3 million units.[12]

This concern can take on many forms, with some Christians stating it's the responsibility of the faith community, not government, to address poverty—as if the faith community can best cheer on those pulling themselves up by the bootstraps as the government steps aside as happened during the Reagan administration.

While there are multiple ways to address this concern, one of the most creative contemporary forms of government assistance is emerging and already demonstrating that it doesn't seem to breed dependence and waste: *guaranteed income programs*. Such programs are not the same as *universal basic income* (programs that seek to fund an entire population irrespective of income levels),

---

12. Dreier, "Reagan's Legacy," paras. 7–8; 12–13.

Poverty: Living without Enough

and typically provide cash assistance to those who are working, who are just above the poverty line, and who don't qualify for typical forms of assistance. Initial results are positive: "A February report by the University of Pennsylvania's Center for Guaranteed Income Research analyzed a program in Cambridge, Massachusetts, that gave $500 a month to single-caretaker households from 2021 to 2023. It found that within one year, 40% were working full time, compared to 28% of a control group." "Reviewing an 18-month pilot in St. Paul, Minnesota, from 2020 to 2022, the researchers found participants' employment rate had hit 63% six months after the program ended, up from 49% when it began."[13]

When we look to government, we need not only look at assistance programs. From my own backyard, the city began to attend to the shortage of affordable housing—part of the context for poverty. Local groups commissioned studies and advanced proposals for zoning changes that ultimately the city commission unanimously adopted.[14] Requirements were changed to allow more accessory dwelling units—small houses on the same property as another home. In addition, the number of unrelated individuals living in the same home was increased from four to six and the opportunity to have from two to six units in a home was given greater feasibility. Requirements for accompanying parking were also relaxed. All of these changes create opportunity for individuals to find affordable housing, thereby increasing the chance to escape poverty.

Why should we care about tax credits and governmental assistance, exploitation and lopsided assistance, and segregation and bifurcation as well as a whole host of other issues, all the way from systems to my neighbor? Listen to God's word.

Two Old Testament passages instruct us to defend and uphold those impoverished. Proverbs 31:9 says, "Speak up and judge fairly; defend the rights of the poor and needy." Psalm 82:3 states, "Defend the weak and fatherless; uphold the cause of the poor and oppressed." Then, in Luke 3:11 we find John the Baptist's response

---

13. McCorvey, "Free Cash Programs," paras. 16–17.
14. Buursma, "GR Makes 'Significant' Changes," paras. 13 and following.

to those coming to him: "John answered, 'Anyone who has two shirts should share with the one who has none, and anyone who has food should do the same.'" Notice the action words: *speak, judge, defend, share.*

Then, turn to Zech 7:9, where we read, "This is what the Lord Almighty said: 'Administer true justice; show mercy and compassion to one another.'" While the first three verses seem to be directed to individuals and/or the church, this verse may be read as a directive to the systems of government back in Old Testament days and now. In other words, our care might be providing a neighbor some clothing, food, or tutoring. But like those advocates who came together around housing in Grand Rapids, we need to focus on the systems so that the administration of justice is advanced through rules and policies that provide a doorway out of poverty.

WHAT YOU CAN DO TO PROMOTE LIFE

I rejoice that I had friends who were part of the faith-based advocacy group that accompanied the housing changes that were adopted in Grand Rapids. Yes, ordinary citizens can make a difference, not just in the voting booth but by advocacy. Matthew Desmond concludes his recent book by calling all of us to advocate for a future of shared prosperity.

I rejoice as well that there are ordinary folks addressing both the antecedents and effects of poverty every day. In our town a community leader created a Community Food Club.[15] Four individuals from our church as well as dozens more pick up unsold food from major retailers each week, bringing it to the Community Food Club where members can buy food with their points instead of dollars. As I mentioned earlier, a small team of folks tutor the refugee family living in our church's Refugee Welcome Home, filling in the gaps to help the children succeed in school. Members of a central city church just a few blocks from our church bought up

---

15. Jones, "Low-Income Grocer Offers Dignity."

dilapidated buildings across from their church, tore them down, and had affordable housing units built.

Notice the word *church* keeps popping up. Certainly, there are other vehicles for believers to pursue pro-life, anti-poverty measures, but the church is one of the most enduring institutions in impoverished neighborhoods. A few decades back, a colleague and I from Calvin University approached a dozen African-American and white church pastors in these neighborhoods, linking them together to create educational opportunities for the neighborhood youth, meeting immediate educational needs in order to help them all the way to college. The Kellogg Foundation and the Ford Foundation saw the potential and funded this effort. True, suburban churches can reach into these areas with projects and partnership, but we must not fail to realize that in most cases, God's church is already there, and we must be there as well.

4

Health and Wellness for Living

My wife, Barb, has taught nursing in some manner for the last forty plus years. The last two decades she has focused on teaching community health, contextualizing her teaching to a specific neighborhood of need. I love her stories and how simple acts such as bringing older women together can enhance a sense of well-being. Of course, the issues are much more complex, and it begins with access to health care.

Teaching at a Christian university, Barb has always focused on access to health care as a human right, not just the privilege of one's ethnicity, economic level, or employment status. However, it was not unusual for her to find comments on her teaching evaluations labeling her a socialist and, therefore, not a Christian!

Thankfully, those comments were few, for most of the students learned the lesson embedded deep in Scripture—that life is precious, and all should have the benefit of the methods for medical intervention when needed, for pharmaceuticals as prescribed, and doorways to health providers at all times.

Let's consult some specific revelation. Jeremiah 30:17 is addressed to the scattered people of Israel: "'But I will restore you to health and heal your wounds,' declares the Lord, 'because you are called an outcast, Zion for whom no one cares.'" While we shouldn't rush to label this as God's endorsement of universal health care, it is instructive because God promises to heal those who are outcasts. God's love and promise of health and healing is focused on those on the margins.

In the New Testament, John offers a prayer in 3 John 1:2: "Beloved, I pray that you may prosper in all things and be in health, just as your soul prospers." The beautiful thing about this prayer is that it is holistic, reminding us that our love to others is not just that their souls would go to heaven, but that they would experience good health. No splitting between body and soul. It reminds me of the beauty when churches employ a parish nurse, ministering to body and soul.

Finally, 1 Cor 6:19-20 encourages us to stay healthy—to keep our bodies healthy: "Do you not know that your bodies are temples of the Holy Spirit, who is in you, whom you have received from God? You are not your own; you were bought at a price. Therefore honor God with your bodies." Of course, we can't meet that responsibility when living in a food desert where fresh fruits and vegetables are missing, when swamped with little children underfoot with no opportunity for childcare, or when gym membership is financially impossible.

Of course, there are thousands of voices relying on general revelation, encouraging us to stay healthy. Why? Some voices do so out of their humanistic commitments, having come to understand the beauty of the human body and to have discovered ways to improve its functioning. Others do so in order that insurance providers—private and governmental—remain viable. It should be no surprise that some insurance companies offer gym membership and others, diet plans. It is in their best interests!

Let's agree on a few things. God's desire, even for the marginalized, is for our health and wellness. God does not make this magically happen, for we read that we have an important role in staying healthy. Many who don't rely on God's word add to that encouragement despite differing rationale.

Be careful, however, before you end up concluding that health and wellness is simply an individual's responsibility. If this is your conclusion, turn in your insurance card and pay for everything out of pocket. No, just as you understand the need to be part of a collective of individuals that find the greatest possible access to health care, your neighbor needs the same. While the insurance card in your purse or wallet might reflect a privilege you earned through education and workplace faithfulness, the Bible makes clear that God's desire is not just that you are healthy, but your neighbor—even the outcast—has the same opportunities to be healthy. In other words, health and wellness is both an individual and a collective responsibility.

These are not two separate responsibilities. As I pointed out before, some individuals are not able to find doorways to health—not because they desire to be unhealthy, but because they don't have access to healthy foods, free time to walk around the block, or resources to exercise during the cold winter months. Even more basic is the issue of access to medical insurance.

In the United States, we have a system unlike many countries who have nationalized health insurance. Our system provides basic governmental care for the very poor and for retirees, while private insurance companies cover (incompletely) the remainder. Through my work with newly arriving refugees per the former and my own retired status, these two governmental efforts—Medicaid and Medicare—provide the basics. Instead of delving into either of both of these plans, better to look at the slice of the US population just above Medicaid cut-offs: those hardly making a livable wage.

It is that slice that the Affordable Care Act (ACA, often referred to as Obamacare) sought, in large part, to address and that requires our attention. Passed in 2010, the goal stated soon after was this:

> When fully implemented, the Act will cut the number of uninsured Americans by more than half. The law will result in health insurance coverage for about 94% of the American population, reducing the uninsured by 31 million people, and increasing Medicaid enrollment by 15 million beneficiaries. Approximately 24 million people are expected to remain without coverage.[1]

---

1. Rosenbaum, "Patient Protection and Affordable Care Act," para. 3.

Thus, a purpose of the act was, in part, to ensure more people were insured. The methods to meet this goal were many but included strategies such as creating the marketplace for inexpensive health insurance that would attract younger people, mandating companies of a certain size or greater would provide health insurance, and the like. But notice, the plan was not universal coverage ("24 million ... without coverage") and while it was to expand coverage for government programs like Medicaid, it was not a new government insurance plan.

So, was the overall goal of providing more people access to health insurance met? Twelve years later, the results show great progress. The Peter G. Peterson Foundation found that "in 2022, 26 million people—or 7.9 percent of the population—were uninsured, according to a report in September 2023 from the Census Bureau."[2] So not quite 24 million uninsured, but close!

Did pro-lifers stand up and cheer? Let's go back to the early days of the Affordable Care Act. Focus on the Family rightly noted that "the ACA allows health-care plans to include abortion coverage [and] it allows states to pass laws prohibiting plans that allow abortion" but then it went on to make a very specific objection: "the ACA requires insurance plans with abortion coverage sold on state exchanges to set up what amounts to an 'abortion slush fund' that collects premiums from every enrollee—regardless of the enrollee's gender, age or view on abortion—to pay for abortions."[3] You see their strategy: ensuring the readers became fearful and even angry that they may have to pay for abortions. While objection to this slush fund may be legitimate, notice that this relates to only those plans with abortion coverage. Stop and think. If you receive coverage through an insurance provider that covers abortions—even if your company may opt out of that portion of the plan—do you think your company and your contributions are segregated in a way that funds are not intermingled with funds from those who opt in on this part of coverage? In other words, did the Affordable Care Act *add* a new dimension or was it

2. Peter G. Peterson Foundation, "Share of Americans," para. 1.
3. Earll, "Abortion and Obamacare," paras. 9 and 11.

simply extending current practice of the insurance companies and remaining consistent with US laws and policies (that no plans are required to cover abortion) at the time? The short answer is no—a new dimension was not added.

Remaining focused on the early days of the Affordable Care Act, why else might have so many, including evangelical Christians, been opposed to the plan? The *American Journal of Medicine* references a 2014 Pew poll which found that "80% of those who *opposed* the *ACA* said a major reason was 'too much government involvement in *health care*.'"[4]

Too much of a role for the government in health care? With further research, we find striking contradictions. Two factors of the Affordable Healthcare Act are actually quite popular: provision for preexisting conditions and allowance for young adults to stay on their family's health insurance until age twenty-six. In terms of the former, 72 percent of respondents of a poll said this provision of the Act was very important to continue, and 51 percent of respondents said the same about the latter.[5]

One wonders if these popular or semi-popular provisions are endorsed because of love of neighbor. Or, might it be to the individual's best interest that his or her preexisting condition doesn't close the door to a job transfer . . . or that a son or daughter recently graduated from college with a job but without health insurance is able to stay on the family's plan a few more years?

So, back to the current question: With such gains in access to health insurance coverage, is the pro-life lobby—including many, many evangelical Christians—cheering the progress made in lowering the number of uninsured Americans? I could find little evidence, for or against. The only possible link is found in the campaign leading up to the 2024 presidential election: "On the campaign trail, former President Donald Trump is once again promising to repeal and replace the Affordable Care Act—a nebulous goal that became one of his administration's splashiest policy failures."[6]

---

4. Dalen et al., "Why Do So Many Oppose," 809.

5. Kirzinger et al., "Five Charts," Figure 2.

6. Rovner, "Repealing the Affordable Care Act?," para. 1.

Health and Wellness for Living

Perhaps all—including evangelical pro-lifers—are finding much of the Affordable Care Act to their liking, but as Donald Trump might also be their preferred candidate, they might join in his objections to the Act. Bottom line: Any embrace of the provisions of the Affordable Care Act by pro-lifers may be related to their own self-interests, and may change with the ways conservative political winds blow. It is doubtful that its accomplishments are resulting in cheers of victory in the National Right to Life offices.

Apart from health insurance, there is another health-related issue we should focus on to promote life and its flourishing: environmental health. From Three Mile Island's radioactive accident decades ago, to more recent discoveries about microplastics and their effect on human well-being, there is an important and significant link between the environment in which we live and human health and well-being. Unlike typical health discussions covering cancer to chicken pox, diabetes to depression, this topic is contextualized to our lived environment.

Listen to the news, and you'll hear stories about PFAs in groundwater and cancer, air quality and asthma, lead paint and childhood disorders. The commonality of these examples, as well as many other things, is that the human impact on aspects of the environment can result in deleterious effects on the population or vulnerable subgroups. For example, many years ago I served as the psychologist at a hospital-based Lead Clinic in our community. Almost without exception, the children I evaluated were from lower socioeconomic status with a great many of them African-American.

While you may ignore some of this because it doesn't affect you personally or at present (but perhaps a prediction for the future), once again, loving your neighbor demands your attention. If you are for life, you need to be aware of a great span of environmental concerns related to health and well-being. The list is seemingly endless, so your vigilance is required. Groundwater, we find, can be easily contaminated by the dumping practices of just a few decades back. Thus, those using such groundwater for drinking or irrigation put themselves and others at risk. Lakes and streams can be polluted, compromising the fish that are caught and introducing potential health risks to those dining on fish. We read stories of such dense air pollution that those in China and India encounter days when it is not safe for their respiratory systems to venture outside; it may be the case that we may be impacting our respiratory systems, even though the air we breathe is not as saturated as that in China or India. But let's be clear: Vulnerable population groups have the greatest risk of environmental harm.

This list could go on and on. But the point, I hope, is clear. To be fully pro-life, one needs to be an environmentalist. Sadly, that is often not the case. According to the Pew Research Center, "Evangelicals . . . also are less inclined than the general public to see climate change as a serious problem, as well as to say various negative consequences are likely to occur in the coming decades because of global warming."[7] Whether attending to God's word and the call in Genesis to be care-takers, or listening to science's dire predictions based on what has been revealed to them, believers—especially pro-life believers—should be first in line, seeking to halt dangerous environmental practices and clamor for restoration and remediation where needed. Instead, there is often suspicion and doubts and wide-scale ignoring of our responsibilities and the signs of danger.

Finally in this chapter we should look at two health-related issues about which pro-lifers need to become more aware: mental health and addictions. First, mental health. The pandemic that began in 2020 seemingly triggered challenges of mental health among youth. Gotlib and colleagues found, when comparing to a control group of pre-pandemic youth, "adolescents assessed after the pandemic shutdowns reported more symptoms of anxiety and depression and greater internalizing problems. Their brains showed thinning of the cortex, which helps execute mental processes like planning and self-control, and reduced volume in the hippocampus and amygdala, which are involved in accessing memories and regulating responses to fear and stress, respectively."[8] The results

---

7. Alper, "Religious Groups' Views," para. 3.
8. Gotlib et al., "COVID-19 Associated," para. 5.

HEALTH AND WELLNESS FOR LIVING

of this study are striking, for the research does not rely only on self-report; it also relates the findings to brain-changes. It is amazing what God reveals to us through science, thereby showing us a responsibility to love our sons and daughters and our neighbors with appropriate care.

It's not only COVID-19 where we see unwelcome changes in mental health among our youth. Those who are struggling with sexual identity issues also demonstrate significant mental health issues, according to a study by Luk and colleagues.

> Relative to heterosexual adolescents, sexual minority adolescents (those who are attracted to the same or both sexes or are questioning; 6.3% of the weighted sample) consistently reported higher depressive symptoms from 11th grade to 3 years after high school. Mediation analyses indicated that sexual minority adolescents reported lower family satisfaction, greater cyberbullying victimization, and increased likelihood of unmet medical needs, all of which were associated with higher depressive symptoms. The mediating role of cyberbullying victimization was more pronounced among male than female participants.[9]

Please note; the issue isn't your biblical hermeneutic nor whether LGBTQ+ individuals may serve as an elder in your church. Your challenge and mine is that a certain number of young people struggle with their sexuality, particularly during adolescence. While we might be more aware of it in today's society, adolescence has always been a key period of development for sexual identity. What might be different today? Greater acceptance in society might lead to greater and riskier exploration of identity. Social media may open greater opportunities for cyberbullying. But my point is this: The challenge among a portion of adolescents has always been with us—it's just more evident today.

I recall a private conversation with the chair of the board of trustees where I served as college president. Coming from a traditional position, he cautioned me about society's growing

---

9. Luk et al., "Sexual Orientation and Depressive Symptoms," para. 3.

acceptance of LGBTQ+ individuals. Noting that homosexuality is a condition, not a choice, I told the board chair a story about one of our students. He was dressing up in drag and frequenting the bars downtown. I suggested that this young man didn't need a sermon; rather, he needed the support of our faculty and other professionals. What kind of support? To tell him what he was doing was fine? No, to help him understand better the sexual identity struggles he was experiencing and what were safe and appropriate ways to better come to terms with himself.

Remember, God's injunction about our neighbor is not tied up in judgment; it's wrapped in love. Whatever the issue—pandemic challenges, sexual identity, or other—we need to respond to all with care and love. While my emphasis here has been on adolescents and youth, we must be fully loving toward all.

One last health issue to address: alcoholism and addiction. Sometimes this is a hidden struggle; other times, it's a struggle that spills over into the lives of loved ones, may involve the criminal justice system, and impacts an individual's employment and relationships. These health-related challenges affect many. We should know a few things about these conditions; first, the role of heredity as summarized by a team at Rutgers University:

> More than half of the differences in how likely people are to develop substance use problems stem from DNA differences, though it varies a little bit by substance. Research suggests alcohol addiction is about 50 percent heritable, while addiction to other drugs is as much as 70 percent heritable.[10]

Thus, we should face alcoholism and addiction not as if it is a choice or character flaw in a selfish individual. No, for many if not most, genetics have predisposed those who struggle with this lifelong challenge. Of course, environmental factors may contribute: Growing up in a home where drugs are used or some early trauma may fuel the causation.

---

10. Smith, "Rutgers Researchers Delve Deep," para. 3.

In addition, we need to realize alcoholism and addiction are chronic diseases, much like diabetes or heart disease; the American Medical Association labeled alcoholism a disease in 1956 and addiction in 1987. Then, "in 2011 the American Society of Addiction Medicine (ASAM) joined the AMA, defining addiction as a chronic brain disorder, not a behavior problem, or just the result of making bad choices"; consider this description of the brain's function:

> Addiction changes the way the brain works, rewiring its structure. Drugs and alcohol hack into your brain's communication system and interfere with how nerve cells send, receive and process information. The brain's reward system activates when we do something we like—eating a piece of our favorite pie, hanging out with friends, or going for a run, for instance. That reward comes in the chemical dopamine. Drugs or alcohol trigger the release of dopamine. Dopamine makes us feel good and want to keep doing what we're doing. It also teaches the brain to repeat the behavior. Cues trigger the reward system, fuel cravings and create a habit loop. The smell of pie baking can make you salivate in anticipation of the taste. Addiction fuels habits too—craving a cigarette every morning with coffee or wanting a hit when you drive past the house where you used to do drugs. When you take a drug, your brain releases a flood of dopamine, much more than it would when you're eating your favorite pie. Your brain overreacts and cuts back on dopamine production to bring it down to a normal level. As you continue to use drugs, your body produces less dopamine. Things that brought you pleasure—that pie, friends, and even drugs—don't anymore. Once you're addicted, it takes more and more drugs just to feel normal.[11]

Truly, it's not as simple as saying "no." There are three basic ways to treat alcoholism: behavioral treatments (focused on counseling), medications, and mutual support groups such as Alcoholics Anonymous. While effectiveness has been shown for all three,

---

11. Indiana University Health, "Is Addiction Really a Disease?," paras. 3–13.

"ultimately, there is no one-size-fits-all solution, and what may work for one person may not be a good fit for someone else."[12]

How can we become champions for life for those struggling with alcoholism and addiction? Consider what Philip Yancey reported from a friend:

> When I'm late to church, people turn around and stare at me with frowns of disapproval. I get the clear message that I'm not as *responsible* as they are. When I'm late to AA, the meeting comes to a halt and everyone jumps up to hug and welcome me. They realize that my lateness may be a sign that I almost didn't make it. When I show up, it proves that my desperate need for them won out over my desperate need for alcohol.[13]

Yancey continues, identifying what we can learn from groups like AA, identifying their emphasis on grace, not perfection. Indeed, whether in church, among one's own family, or in society, we should meet the person struggling with alcoholism or addiction with two-fold grace: pointing them to grace-filled groups and extending our own grace. Extending our own grace may mean the combination of unconditional love and a willingness to stand by the one we love when it's time to start over—again. Research reveals to us that instead of following the advice to step away and let a loved one hit "rock bottom," "addiction experts say providing support is more likely to lead to someone entering recovery."[14]

WHAT YOU CAN DO TO PROMOTE LIFE

Imagine yourself in a conversation with a friend. The subject turns to the Affordable Care Act, or to addictions, or to snacking. Don't respond by telling them they are wrong. Rather, ask them why they hold that view or do what they do; you might get a complete

---

12. National Institute on Alcohol Abuse and Alcoholism, "Treatment for Alcohol Problems," paras. 10–13.

13. Yancey, "Lessons from Rock Bottom," para. 7.

14. Becker, "This Family Didn't Wait," para. 1.

story or just a grunt. Your aim is not to convince the other, but speak to why you uphold the sanctity of life in matters of health. Maybe your story is as simple as how grateful you are that your young adult son can still be on your health plan while he searches for a post-college job. Perhaps you have a story of someone who struggles with addiction—certainly not of her own choosing—and how you remain supportive. Just maybe you hate vegetables, too, so you explain how yogurt-covered raisins have replaced Doritos in your cupboard.

May 1 John 4:7–8 be our guide as we provide understanding, access, and intervention to those who experience health challenges: "Dear friends, let us love one another, for love comes from God. Everyone who loves has been born of God and knows God. Whoever does not love does not know God, because God is love."

5

Disability: Lives Not to Be Overlooked

IT WAS A SUNDAY morning, about twenty-five years ago. A new professor in town, her husband, and two children were being welcomed at our church. And the welcome was to include the baptism of their son with Down Syndrome, who was about seven or eight years old. However, Gabriel, their son, had no interest in leaving the pew nor to join his family members up front for the welcome and baptism. He was not going to move! After what must have seemed to be an interminable amount of time to Gabriel's parents but probably was less than a minute or two, something unscripted and unprompted happened. Our son Paul, also with Down Syndrome and about twelve or thirteen at the time, left where we were sitting, walked over to Gabriel, took his hand, and led him, without any protest, to join his family in the front of church.

    It was an amazing moment, and we all witnessed a few critical things. First, these two youngsters with Down Syndrome could relate to each other. No words were needed, no instruction given. Only a hand of friendship given in love. Clearly, a wonderful display that they were both children of God, beautifully reflecting the love of their Creator. Second, Paul hardly knew Gabriel at the time, but preexisting friendship wasn't needed to be neighborly; no words of encouragement were needed. I don't know how Paul's mind was working that morning, but it must have been something as simple as "Gabriel needs my help, so I will help him." No measuring the cost of helping, no review of the rules of decorum in

Disability: Lives Not to Be Overlooked

our worship service, no permission from Mom and Dad needed. It was time to help out a new neighbor. And third, the context was baptism. What better time to understand how God values each one of us than at that moment. When God claims us as our own, it doesn't relate to intelligence, finances, gender, ethnicity, or the like. It's pretty simple. God loves each of his children, as so should we.

But, it hasn't been always the case. Not so long ago, those with disabilities[1] were relegated to institutions, unable to be assured of education, and sometimes even subjected to experimental and dangerous procedures. But in the last number of decades, things have been changing, as God's "most elegant book" has led many to new understandings time and time again.

De-institutionalization became the first of a number of sweeping changes in the last few decades of the previous century. Prompted by the Community Mental Health Act of 1963[2] and other social forces, de-institutionalization was based on the belief that lives were better lived in communities, not in institutions. Some criticized these changes, as the communities people moved into were either not willing to accept them or ready for them. Some group homes were met with resistance, with neighbors shouting "not in my backyard!" Some with mental illness ended up on the streets, as the homeless population grew. Yet others laud the successes of these changes, noting that group homes with a small number of residents were far better than the masses held in institutions. Then, in 1975, President Gerald Ford signed the Individuals with Disabilities Act (IDEA) into law; more on the impact of IDEA on education later. Then, in 1990, the Americans with Disabilities Act was signed, and it "prohibits discrimination against people with disabilities in several areas, including employment, transportation, public accommodations, communications and access to state and local government."[3]

---

1. In this chapter, I refer to those with disabilities, most often focusing on those whose primary disability is in the cognitive or intellectual realm. At times, I will use an alternative term, those with *special needs*.

2. Erickson, "Deinstitutionalization through Optimism," paras. 1–2.

3. United States Department of Labor, "Americans with Disabilities Act," para. 1.

Studies can only partially lead us to understanding the results. I'd like to think the hypothesis that people—particularly those with disabilities and mental illness—will have a better quality of life in the community than in an institution is a God-given revelation. Study after study has sought to measure outcomes, but in the final analysis, it is only possible to trust that the sanctity of human life is best found in community. Unlike the scientific approach I outlined in the first chapter, it is not possible to test what's best for a given individual, for living in an institution or in community defies the with/without study approach. One cannot put an individual in one setting for a few weeks, then another for a few more weeks and then another. One might call this jerking someone around, and if you know anyone who is disabled or struggles with mental illness, a lack of consistency is never a good thing.

Rather, we can only understand individual lives in sequence. One such sequence came home to me over a couple of decades. My aunt and uncle adopted a baby boy when I was around four. As my parents told me, the delays in my cousin's development were significant and of great concern to the adoption agency. Finally, despite my aunt and uncle's objections, they revoked the adoption and placed this child in a state-run institution.

While I was in college, I was a summer camp counselor, and this included taking a group of teens to an island for a week-long camping adventure. One of the teens was a young man who obviously had challenges. Intellectually, he seemed to be somewhat challenged, and his gait was more of a shuffle. In fact, because of his poor coordination, he tumbled down a sand dune cliff one day; thankfully, he wasn't injured.

I remained curious about this young man and sought to learn more about him. I found that he had lived in an institution, and, only a few years before joining me on that summer camping expedition, had moved into a group home. Ah-ha, that clumsy, uncoordinated gait was probably acquired from living in the institution, I concluded. But then an even bigger ah-ha moment: that young man was my cousin whose adoption by my aunt and uncle had been revoked!

Disability: Lives Not to Be Overlooked

I learned also that he had made good gains by moving into the community, living in the group home, and going to a school that included special education services. But what if he had remained in my aunt and uncle's family? Is not family the best form of community in which a child can grow and flourish?

I trust revoking an adoption due to a cognitive disability would not occur today as it did then. But I also have heard of situations where the family may have knowingly or unknowingly adopted a special needs child, only to find later (in adolescence, for some) they were unable to continue with this child in their family. Such sadness!

My point is this. I believe the hypothesis that communities are better than institutions and a family setting is best if it is at all possible. I believe the hypothesis because I see God's hand in his design for individuals with disabilities and with their families.

God is not silent in explaining to us the value he places upon those with disabilities. You may recall the deep, deep friendship between Jonathan and David in the Old Testament. When Jonathan was killed in battle, the caregiver and Jonathan's five-year old son, Mephibosheth, fled in haste, and in so doing, Mephibosheth was injured, leaving him unable to walk. Fast forward, and we read in 2 Sam 9:7 and following that King David asked if anyone from Jonathan's family remained alive. Soon, he learned that Mephibosheth was living, so King David had him brought to him: "'Don't be afraid,' David said to him, 'for I will surely show you kindness for the sake of your father Jonathan. I will restore to you all the land that belonged to your grandfather Saul, and you will always eat at my table.'"

I don't know for sure how big the king's table was, how many people usually gathered around it for a meal, and if David was always present. But it's important to understand that David included him—his friend's disabled son—into his home and at his table, restoring to him that which was rightfully his. Mephibosheth is not forgotten, and he's now included in the household of King David. Yes, I believe the story tells us something about God's love for this disabled young man and his design for transforming lives.

Back to contemporary policy: Our role is to welcome those with disabilities—including in group homes and our individual homes—into our communities and congregations. Individuals with disabilities need our support and love, and their parents do as well as they face multiple challenges and hurdles unique to special needs children and teens. Moreover, our experience has shown that our church and extended family were the key providers of support and encouragement as we have needed it.

I think back to when Paul was a baby in heart failure, needing to be tube fed every two hours or so. If not for Barb's mother and our fellow church member Mary learning how to gavage feed Paul, we would never have had a break. I remember when Paul was in elementary school. The best educational option available for him was three times the cost of the private Christian education each of our other children was receiving. Our minister and elder came over to tell us that the church was stepping in and would take over the financial responsibility for Paul's education, for as they explained, the congregation took its baptism vows to Paul seriously.

Speaking of schools, another significant shift in the last few decades of the previous century was the mandate that public schools were required to provide special education, as mentioned earlier. Called PL 94-142, President Gerald Ford signed it into law back in 1975. It required, among other things, educational planning for each specific individual and a continuum of services within schools so that children could be educated in the least restrictive environment. This new law "was a response to Congressional concern for two groups of children: the more than 1 million children with disabilities excluded entirely from the education system and the children with disabilities who had only limited access to the education system, and were therefore denied an appropriate education. This latter group comprised more than half of all children with disabilities who were living in the U.S. at that time."[4]

This law has been reauthorized a number of times and has led us to the current emphasis on inclusion. The Act originally posited

---

4. United States Department of Education, "History of Individuals," paras. 6 and 9.

something called "the least restrictive environment," which led to a process of asking questions such as "would this child do best in a special segregated school, in a regular school but in a self-contained (segregated) classroom, or in a regular school and regular classroom but with pull-outs for specialized instruction?" The current focus on inclusion upends such questions and simply notes that all special needs children and youth are best educated when they are included in regular education. With this foundation, there have evolved a number of ways to give specialized instruction, the chief of which are alongside in the classroom or pulled-out for individual teaching. Again, glimmers of God's design for children and youth shine through. The basic hypothesis, difficult to prove beyond a shadow of doubt, reflects best what we know about all children—what they all need and what they individually need.

In our case, we have had the best of both worlds. Paul's K–9 schooling was via inclusion. He had a homeroom filled with a number of buddies each year and was pulled out for specialized instruction. We have often said that this helped him to learn academically as well as how to participate socially.

Then, just as he started high school, we moved to Chicago and very close to us was a Christian special education school that emphasized job preparation in the high school years. While he was included only with others with disabilities, his education was individualized, helping him to develop job skills, both in general and in specific areas via job try-outs. This approach worked beautifully, and after graduation, Paul began working in food service, first on the campus of Trinity Christian College and currently at the Frederick Meijer Gardens.

Why is Paul successful in the work place? Both approaches served to help him become a basic reader, important for notes and signage in the work place. Inclusion helped him understand how to participate in a group of workers. Specialized vocational training helped him develop job skills necessary for food service as well as how to appropriately serve the customers. (And we continue to periodically utilize the services of a job coach when changes come his way in the job setting.)

Indeed, the world has changed for those with disabilities and the rest of us who include them in our families, schools, workplaces, churches, and communities. One could label this as a time of transformation; I consider it a point in time at which general revelation has broken through to the benefit of all. In many ways, I believe this inclusion reflects similar transformation that we read about many times in the New Testament, as Christ would turn his attention to a person with a disability and miraculously transform the person.

Transformation isn't only for the person with a disability. We can be transformed as well. A movie about schizophrenia touches on how our ideas about those with disability are transformed. Alicia Nash, the wife of the brilliant yet schizophrenic John Nash, says, "I think often what I feel . . . is obligation. Or guilt over wanting to leave. Rage against John, against God and—But . . . then I look at him . . . and I force myself to see the man that I married. And he becomes that man. He's transformed into someone that I love. And I'm transformed into someone who loves him."[5] Transformation in both directions!

So why bring up disabilities as I seek to stretch the focus of pro-life brothers and sisters? Three reasons. First, not everybody on the pro-life bandwagon allows those with disabilities to come on board. I know of some churches where those with disabilities are ignored. Contrast that with how we chose our church in Chicago. After visiting a number of churches and greetings always aimed and Barb and me, at Loop Church we entered in the back, and Jim reached out to Paul—having never met him nor assessed his abilities—and asked him to participate in the service by handing things out. Our church shopping stopped and we stayed at Loop Church as long as we lived in the Chicago area. Similarly, while our son Paul has been very fortunate in employment, we know far too many of his friends who, at best, can only find part-time volunteer positions.

Second, back to the issue of abortion. Apart from my push to first define the beginning of life, we must also realize that abortion

---

5. Howard, *Beautiful Mind*.

disproportionately takes the lives of those unborn fetuses with disabilities. The National Institutes of Health tell us that "termination rates range from 67% to 85% among the overall population of individuals with a positive prenatal diagnosis of Down Syndrome."[6] While this statistic doesn't provide additional information such as number of weeks gestation, cases where the mother's life was endangered, or the like, clearly it is a highly disturbing trend. Despite all of the progress detailed in the preceding paragraphs, it is evident that in one area of disability, Down Syndrome, a super majority of parents fail to see God's image reflected in these fetuses, and deny them life.

Finally, I would so appreciate pro-life believers to support, in tangible ways, the fostering and adoption of children with disabilities. Looking carefully at foster care, one author has found that "children with disabilities constantly struggle with being adopted with many living out their childhood and teenage years in the foster care system until they age out. Youth with special needs who age out of the foster care system are more likely to be unemployed, more likely to be homeless or impoverished, and less likely to pursue a higher education."[7] Other authors find that there are over 130,000 special needs (a term in the adoption literature that often includes more than just those with disabilities) children waiting for adoption.[8] Furthermore, the incidence of disability or multiple disabilities among adopted children is two to two and a half times higher than other adopted children.[9] Clearly, there is an overabundance of special needs children in the foster care system and among those waiting for adoption; these children should be as loudly advocated for and supported by pro-life advocates as the unborn, for these "neighbors," too, bear the image of God.

Those with disability are needed in our society. If you know a child or adult with disabilities, you will understand unconditional acceptance. Instead of judgment or standoffishness, you'll see a

6. Chaiken et al., "Association between Rates," para. 13.
7. Stogsdill, "Children with Disabilities," 5.
8. Lile, "Adopting a Child," para. 1.
9. Grcevich, "What Are the Stats?," para. 5.

smile or receive a hug. Often we see limitations instead of the possibilities. Often we wonder about their worth and fail to see their contributions. In Paul's case, he has made an impact in a surprising way.

When we adopted our children from Ethiopia, Getenet was fifteen. Among the host of adjustment questions he faced, he repeatedly came to us with his observation about his new brother Paul. Getenet would say, "He's not disabled, is he?" Getenet was comparing Paul—observing his strong social skills, his independence, and his work skills—with his experiences with similar young people in Ethiopia. In his home country, Getenet told us that those with special needs were often hidden with no opportunities for school or employment. He explained that often families thought a special needs child was, at best, a reason to be shamed and, at worst, the result of a curse. Getenet was fundamentally amazed at the difference.

In Getenet's first year at Trinity Christian College he signed up for a January term class on disability—not because of an interest, but because it was one of the few courses still open when he registered. But God's plan was to use this class, led by an adjunct professor from Joni and Friends, to further open Getenet's eyes to the possibilities for those with disabilities—those created in God's image just like the rest of us. The instructor had been to Ethiopia and connected with Getenet, helping him more clearly define the need for special education in his home country.

As a result, while still a college student, Getenet began a Christian special education school named Faith School in Addis Ababa! Did he become a special education major? No, he remained focused on his math and physics major. But he took a few trips back home to find the personnel and the place to start the school. At the time it started, it was only the second special education school in this city of more than five million! A few years after its start, the local newspaper featured Getenet's story and included a picture of Paul and Getenet together, with this quote: "'My brother Paul has set a good example to many others and to me,' he said. 'He always impresses me. The Ethiopian people will change through education too.'"[10] This picture of college graduate Getenet—Faith School Founder—and Paul, his inspiration, sums it up!

FIGURE 2

Today, Faith School continues to flourish, educating primarily disabled children from families on the margins—those unable to afford tuitions but in desperate need of opportunities for their children. And, hopefully, Ethiopian society is changing to be more accepting and inclusive of those with special needs.

Each person—including those with disabilities—is made in God's image. I'd like to think that because of this, we reflect characteristics of our Creator. Those with artistic gifts are able to show the creativity of our creating God. Those who respond to others with love and kindness demonstrate the love of the Father. Those who are patient, never giving up, reflect the faithfulness of God. All of these statements, and more, are true, too, for those with disabilities. To close this chapter, one last story is required, for it

10. Holst, "College Student Starts School," 82.

reflects the trust, care, and love of our God between our son Paul and Gabriel, who we met at the beginning of the chapter—but to understand the story, we need to first back up thirty-five plus years ago.

When Paul was born, he had some holes in the chambers of his heart and one common valve instead of two separate mitral and tricuspid valves. By five months, he was in heart failure. We fed him every two or three hours, often gavage feeding him with a tube. But despite our best efforts to bring him to a weight necessary for open heart surgery, we were unsuccessful, and heart surgery needed to proceed.

The surgeon created two valves out of one, and we dodged a bullet for thirty-six years. But then, Paul's condition deteriorated rapidly, as his surgically fashioned valve no longer was effective. Thus, it was time again for surgery at the same hospital where he had had his first surgery thirty-six years before. However in those intervening years, the science of heart surgery had grown by leaps and bounds (again, giving witness to God's general revelation), and a team of both pediatric and adult cardiac specialists greeted us. The surgery to insert an artificial valve went well, but recovery had some challenges—a couple where we thought we were going to lose Paul. But God was good, and Paul slowly recovered, spending a month in the hospital.

Visiting him in the hospital one late afternoon were Gabriel and his parents. Gabriel had by then grown into a fine young man, but to most ears seemed to be largely nonverbal. Thus, this time of visitation was not one rich in conversation between two buddies. Rather it was a time that demonstrated faithfulness and care. Of course, together the parents talked and the long medical journey was explained. And then, as Gabriel and his parents departed, I distinctly heard Gabriel say, "Get better Paul!" Those three words, coming from Gabriel, spoke volumes of what God does in the lives of those with disabilities. We only need to sharpen our ears to hear and our eyes to see the sanctity of life as displayed by Gabriel, Paul, and so many more.

WHAT YOU CAN DO TO PROMOTE LIFE

Whether your friend who supports abortion does so out of a clear understanding of the beginning of life or does so out of a woman's right to make decisions about her own body, it may be helpful to share the statistic about the higher prevalence of those with Down Syndrome being aborted. For me, this statistic is the best way to look at abortion that supersedes perspectives on a woman's right to make her own decisions. Truly, this is a case of society—albeit one woman at a time—trying to rid itself of an entire group of people by keeping them from birth.

Beyond the abortion issue, there are thousands of ways to promote life for those with disabilities. Consider how your church can be more inclusive; might a person with disabilities be an adjunct deacon, assisting in taking the collection Sunday mornings? Consider how your own children might develop to be more understanding and caring adults by enrolling them in a school with an inclusive program for those with disabilities. Consider ways in which your workplace could include those with disabilities, from a simple greeter position to a multitude of other roles that will be performed faithfully and without complaint!

6

Seeking Life in a Culture of Gun Violence

ONE AFTERNOON WE HEARD firecrackers—or so we thought—while our neighbors celebrated a daughter's birthday in their backyard. Cliff explained later that he had simply been shooting his gun up in the air to achieve the same effect. Imagine, pulling out a gun to use in a celebration of another year of life!

An important way to begin a look at the United States' culture of gun violence is to first compare ourselves to other countries. Then, we'll look at some further statistics about the situation within the United States and close by addressing some common perspectives and searching for answers.

> In 2017, U.S. civilians held an average of 120.5 firearms per 100 people, the highest rate in the world by a factor of more than two, followed by Yemen (52.8), Montenegro (39.1), Serbia (39.1) and Uruguay (34.7), according to data from the Small Arms Survey, an independent research project located at the Graduate Institute of International and Development Studies in Geneva, Switzerland. In other words: The United States was the only country with more civilian-held guns than citizens.[1]

Why might this be? Are we a country that has devolved into lawlessness and constant strife such as Yemen? Or, are we hunters extraordinaire, needing to shoot wildlife to put food on our tables?

---

1. Gilligan, "U.S. Remains an Outlier," para. 3.

Seeking Life in a Culture of Gun Violence

The Pew Research Center has provided a helpful study that helps us begin to understand our society and our neighbor, Cliff. First, the descriptive statistics: 40 percent of men and 25 percent of women report owning a gun. Nearly half (47 percent) of those living in rural areas report owning a gun compared to 30 percent in the suburbs and 20 percent in urban areas. In terms of ethnicity, 38 percent of white Americans, 24 percent of African-Americans, 20 percent of Hispanic Americans, and 10 percent of Asian Americans report owning firearms.[2] Why are white Americans the group with the largest percentage of firearm ownership? Is it fear and, if so, what is at the root of such fear?

If we look at these statistics, it is unavoidable to conclude that of those reporting to own a firearm, in many cases ownership must involve not just one firearm but many firearms. So why do more than a third of United States citizens own a firearm—and, in some cases, many firearms?

Schaeffer posits it is nested in the Constitution's Second Amendment—the right to bear arms. In 2008, the Supreme Court provided this interpretation in the majority opinion as they ruled 5–4 on a District of Columbia case: "The Second Amendment protects an individual right to possess a firearm unconnected with service in a militia, and to use that arm for traditionally lawful purposes, such as self-defense within the home."[3] And the research reported on by Schaeffer notes that nearly 75 percent of respondents identify self-protection as their reason for owning a firearm; only about a third report ownership for hunting or sport shooting. So back to the fact that the greatest percentage of gun ownership is among white Americans. If three-fourths of them own a gun(s) for self-defense, what makes them so fearful? Is that what privilege brings?

Why do so many feel unsafe and resort to a firearm, especially compared to other countries? Returning to Gilligan's report, only Columbia, Brazil, and Mexico had higher rates of gun deaths than the United States. Further, Gilligan reports from 2014 to 2020, US

---

2. Schaeffer, "Key Facts about Americans," para. 5.
3. National Constitution Center, "On This Day," para. 2.

deaths due to firearms rose by 35 percent.⁴ From the armchair, it appears that something circular is going on: more guns, more deaths, more fear, more guns, and on and on.

Before continuing on, we need to look more closely at the Second Amendment. Former Chief Justice Warren Burger provided significant focus. Burger authored a piece for the Associated Press in 1991 in which he said "the very language of the Second Amendment refutes any argument that it was intended to guarantee every citizen an unfettered right to any kind of weapon he or she desires. In referring to a 'well regulated militia,' the Framers clearly intended to secure the right to bear arms essentially for military purposes."⁵ Yet, we continue to use a more expansive understanding of the Second Amendment.

So back to fear. Believing fear gives rise to the United States' preoccupation with guns, what might feed such fear? While the contributors may be many, one key factor might be mass shootings—occasions of much media coverage and dreadful consequences. In 2016, forty-nine were killed at a gay nightclub in Orlando, Florida, at that point the United States' deadliest mass-shooting in modern times.⁶ But then, one year later, an even deadlier mass shooting in Las Vegas killed fifty-nine and injured more than five hundred.⁷ Imagine the many tourists and, within a moment, life ends or is changed forever.

If putting oneself in the shoes of unsuspecting Las Vegas tourists or nightclub patrons may be a stretch for some, consider the fifth deadliest mass shooting in the United States—forty-six killed or injured at the First Baptist Church of Sutherland Springs, Texas.⁸ Yes, a church—a place of worship and sanctuary. Fear becomes real. Recent history, too, reminds us that one's ethnicity can become a target as in Pittsburgh's Tree of Life Synagogue shooting

---

4. Gilligan, "U.S. Remains an Outlier," para. 6.
5. Burger, "Second Amendment Has Been Distorted," 13.
6. Zambelich and Hurt, "Three Hours in Orlando," para. 1.
7. Belson et al., "Burst of Gunfire," para. 1.
8. Montgomery et al., "Gunman Kills at Least 26," para. 1.

in 2018[9] or the supermarket shooting in Buffalo, New York, in 2022.[10]

Mass shooting at schools prompt a different kind of fear: fear for innocent children. In the United States, our shared memories go back to Columbine—twenty-five years past as of April 2024. More than a dozen were killed, and our collective ease of sending our children to school each day was shattered. Sadly, in the ensuing twenty-five years, mass shootings at schools have continued to occur: Sandy Hook, Uvalde, and other names continue to live in our memories. The range of shootings have spanned the entire continent, and public schools and Christian schools, alike, have been the sites of such savagery.

Beyond the initial shock and grief, it is curious to see how we, as a society, respond in follow-up. In Uvalde, where nineteen students and two teachers were killed by the gunman, the public outcry skipped to the police: Why had they done nothing for an hour before they entered the building? An important question, but it shouldn't overshadow more significant questions: What led the shooter to resort to this act of murder? How was it possible for the gunman to legally purchase two assault rifles just days before the shooting?[11]

Assault rifles are a particular evil in this madness. The person with an assault rifle can switch between semi-automatic and automatic firing, leading to the seemingly unending spray of bullets used in mass shootings. Why would someone need this kind of weapon? At one time Congress decided they should ban assault weapons, passing the Public Safety and Recreational Firearms Use Protection Act in 1994. Yet, ten years later, when it expired, there was not a majority capable of renewing it. Interestingly, at least one poll found the majority of Americans support such a ban:

> A survey done this month by Morning Consult and Politico found 7 in 10 voters, including 54% of Republicans, supported "a ban on assault-style weapons." Even higher

---

9. Robertson et al., "11 Killed in Synagogue Massacre," para. 1.
10. Deliso et al., "Suspect Fired 50 Rounds," para. 1.
11. Oxner, "Uvalde Gunman Legally Bought," para. 1.

percentages supported a ban on high-capacity magazines and a purchase age of at least 21 for any gun. The survey, done Aug. 5–7, included 1,960 interviews and had a margin of error of two percentage points.[12]

As of January 1, 2024, the State of Illinois has instituted such a ban, successfully resisting a number of court challenges before its implementation. A report, however, finds compliance challenging, particularly with those having possession of such weapons prior to the ban now required to register the weapons.[13]

Other ways society has tried to address these shootings has been to institute laws allowing firearms to be taken from a person when "red flags" are observed as well as placing steps of review—background checks—for firearm purchase. Red flag laws "allow people to petition for the temporary confiscation of an individual's firearms if that person is deemed to be a risk to themselves or to others."[14] The petitioning requires a law enforcement officer (or in a few states, the petitioner can be from roles other than law enforcement) going before a judge to make the case for confiscation whereupon the judge makes a decision. Additionally, some states have instituted background checks when a person seeks to purchase a firearm and/or require licenses to purchase a gun. A recent review by the University of Michigan's Institute for Firearm Injury Prevention found "when implemented properly, background checks at point of sale keep those prohibited from possessing a firearm from obtaining one. However, states that adopt these laws do not necessarily see a decrease in rates of violence, indicating inadequate implementation processes. Purchaser licensing laws, however, see more robust decreases in firearm violence rates."[15]

Beyond bans, red flag laws, and background checks, it is instructive to look at the ensuing attempts at justice after school shootings. In Oxford, Michigan, a fifteen-year-old male killed four students and injured others with a semi-automatic handgun his

12. Elving, "Why Did It Expire?," para. 42.
13. Degman, "Illinois Has Banned Assault Weapons," para. 1.
14. Chasan, "What Are Red Flag," para. 6.
15. Barnes, "Firearm Access Policies Are Effective," para. 10.

Seeking Life in a Culture of Gun Violence

parents had bought him just four days before the November 30, 2021, shooting. After this young man was sentenced to life without parole, his parents have had charges brought before them and both have been convicted of manslaughter and sentenced to prison—seemingly a first case where parents have been held responsible.[16]

If this case is a harbinger of things to come, addressing the actions (purchasing a gun) and inactions (e.g., failure to address mental health issues) of parents in the judicial system may become more frequent. But will this be a deterrent to parents? Will this result in fewer school shootings?

If you're neither a legislator or judge, you may wonder where you fit in this debate. Perhaps it's best for all of us to look at the gun culture in which we live. For me, it's symbolized by this sign—a picture I took in western Michigan during the 2020 presidential campaign. I am puzzled how "God, Guns, and Country" fit together, other than a string of commitments promoted by candidates and their supporters. This string of words, however, evidences how deeply embedded guns are in our culture, and even for Christians.

FIGURE 3

How did the possession of firearms become so deeply embedded in our culture among believers and so many more? Unlike many nations around the world, the United States developed with an extreme individualistic culture. Different from the collective

---

16. Guevara and Ortiz, "James Crumbley, Father."

or community-focused cultures of Africa and Europe, in the US, some aspects of our history have unintentionally contributed to this "me" culture.

For instance, unlike many countries where space is at a premium and community cooperation is required, in its first one hundred years, westward expansion gave individuals the opportunity to establish each their own space—no neighbors, but a great need to be self-sufficient.

In addition, the American Revolution led to a sense of pride and accomplishment in what this rag-a-tag group could do. This War for Independence was focused on the birth of a nation, but this striving for independence grew to characterize its people as well.

Along the way, firearms became companion to this spirit. Whether for protection from wild animals or to drive the Indians farther and farther west, having a firearm became part of the independence package.

My hypothesis is that this gun culture is found among Christians only because they are part of the larger history and culture. In other words, I don't think there's anything uniquely Christian about a style of living that includes a gun. It is simply a case of Christians reflecting the culture at large.

So, back to the political banner. I hope you recognize that the three words—"God, Guns, and Country"—are only words strung together by a political strategist who recognizes that Christianizing this gun culture could be a benefit in reaching some Christian voters. I also doubt that the attempted assassination attempt with an assault rifle on candidate and former president Trump in July of 2024 will change the strategy or the minds of those deeply at home in such a culture.

But when I turn to the Bible, the use of weapons in the Old Testament doesn't seem to have saved Israel (one of the most convincing passages of the God who saves is when David uses a sling and stones), and the message of the New Testament comes from Jesus in Matt 26:52: "'Put your sword back in its place,' Jesus said to him, 'for all who draw the sword will die by the sword.'" Isaiah 2:4 provides the promise that unites the Old and New Testaments: "He

Seeking Life in a Culture of Gun Violence

will judge between the nations and will settle disputes for many peoples. They will beat their swords into plowshares and their spears into pruning hooks. Nation will not take up sword against nation, nor will they train for war anymore."

Yearn for the days when our guns will be melted down into plows and pruning hooks. Please do not conflate gun rights with God. With the coming of Christ, we learn in John 14:27 that he has provided us a gift: "Peace I leave with you; my peace I give you. I do not give to you as the world gives. Do not let your hearts be troubled and do not be afraid."

Be counter-cultural if this is the group you find yourself in. You don't have to put "Outlaw Guns" on your bumper. But when approaching elections, you should search out candidates who are honest about searching for ways to diminish gun violence. You should recognize the horrors that loosened gun control has brought—the countless loss of lives. And you should speak the truth that simplistic gun worship is not the culture in which Christ's light is seen.

Now, more specifically, actions. For I'd like us to proceed through a number of considerations that I believe faithful, pro-life believers should address.

First, where I come from, shooting deer is not only a sport, but necessary for keeping the wild deer population in check, and, for some, it puts food on the table. It seems that having a rifle or two for such purposes is logical, as long as it is securely stored during the off season. The same observation could be made about all kinds of hunting. It might be said that firearms used for hunting do not diminish, maim, or destroy human life.

Second, if you are pro-life, join with me in agreeing that assault weapon bans such as have been instituted in the State of Illinois promote life. I cannot think of any instance, apart from policing and the military, where an ordinary citizen needs an assault weapon. If you are pro-life, I hope you will agree with me, decry the uses of assault weapons in mass shootings, and advance bans such as is law in the State of Illinois.

Third, we need to address fear. I recall a bumper sticker that said "When Guns Are Outlawed, Only Outlaws Will Have Guns."

That's the fear. And that's why many ordinary folks—the simple majority of whom are white Americans—have firearms: for self-protection. The U.S. Department of Justice's Office of Justice Programs includes in its library of documents a study by the National Rifle Association. This report finds that more criminals are killed or wounded each year by citizens using their personal firearm than by the police.[17]

Is this fear warranted? Compare living in the suburbs to the central city—is there a difference in the need for self-defense? Are you a single woman leaving your workplace late at night and walking to your car? The questions can go on and on. But before coming to a quick conclusion about needing a firearm, consider what else can contribute to your safety. A can of pepper spray or a similar spray repellent might be good to carry. If you're walking alone at night, might an escort be available? The possibilities are numerous.

For a number of years we lived in the central city where poverty was epidemic, drug dealing could be found on many corners, break-ins were common, and killings all too frequent. What was our response? Because hot summer nights required windows to be open, we had devices in the main floor windows that limited the opening of the window. We were vigilant about locking doors but never had an alarm system. Instead of buying a firearm, we bought a dog.

Did we live in fear after a handful of break-ins? No, while we felt violated, we realized they most often occurred when we were gone. One night, however, the dog started barking, so I got up to see what was happening. Two or three policemen were crouched on our front porch. Did I wake up the family? No, I quieted the dog and went back to sleep. Law enforcement was ever so much more effective than I could ever be, making me determined to avoid the response of fear.

Perhaps you live in a similar situation, and you have a firearm. Now you have a very important challenge. If you believe you need immediate access to that firearm in the middle of the night,

---

17. National Rifle Association, "Gun Ownership Provides," para. 1.

for example, how will you also keep it inaccessible especially to children in your home? For we hear story after story of children finding a firearm that is unfortunately loaded, and the results are deadly. Consider the findings of Wilson and colleagues:

> The majority (85.5%) of victims were fatally injured at a house or apartment, including 55.6% in their own home. Among all child victims of unintentional fatal firearm injuries, the most common precipitating circumstances were the shooter playing with or showing the firearm to another person (66.6%); unintentionally pulling the trigger (21.3%); thinking the firearm was unloaded, the safety was engaged, or the magazine was disengaged (20.5%); and mistaking the firearm for a toy (10.6%; most commonly among children aged 0–5 years [28.0%]).[18]

WHAT YOU CAN DO TO PROMOTE LIFE

Imagine yourself sitting next a fellow church member who has just explained why guns are important to him and to all. This needs to be a delicate conversation. Of the following questions, consider asking just one or two. Do the costs and risks of owning a firearm outweigh your need for a firearm? Are there kinds of firearms you think should be reserved only for law enforcement and the military? How do we stop the seemingly endless mass killings at schools and other places? Can you wrap your head around former Chief Justice Warren Burger's understanding of the Second Amendment?

Perhaps one of the questions will lead to a respectful conversation. Your witness needs to focus on protecting life, and you may wish to provide your viewpoint that, in many cases, firearms among the citizenry only hasten death most often, rather than promoting life. Promote peace, protect life.

---

18. Wilson et al., "Unintentional Firearm Injury Deaths," para. 6.

7

Racism: A Sin That Diminishes Life

MARRIED AND A DAD, our Ethiopian son drove each day about fifteen miles to work, going through the suburb in which I grew up. It was not uncommon for a police cruiser to pick up his trail as he entered the suburb and follow him nearly all the way to work. Why? The only conclusion we could draw is that he was black, driving through a predominantly white suburb.

Racism perpetuates a disregard for life, turning a person created in God's image into a statistic at best and a target at worst. In our transracial family, the accompanying police cruiser is just one of many instances our two youngest sons have encountered. One of the most biting was while they were in high school and played on the soccer team. One late afternoon, at the conclusion of the game, our two sons did not take part in the closing activity of shaking hands with members of the opposing team. The athletic director instructed the (Hispanic) coach to bench them for the next game. Why? What neither we nor the coach knew at the time—but the AD and assistant coach knew—was that our sons were repeatedly taunted on the pitch, with those from the other team referring to them with the n-word. Our sons had a reason not to shake hands.

The next day, a mother of one of the players from the opposing team called our sons' high school, apologizing for those on the team who taunted our sons. By that time, we knew the full story and the coach called us up to learn what had happened. He was incensed—that the AD had withheld the ugly reason behind our sons' refusing to shake hands, that his assistant coach stayed silent, that the AD had our sons benched, and that he was the last to know. Racism turns a person created in God's image into a target; when others sit by silently, failing to call out racism, racism seemingly wins.

Of course, racism isn't new in our society. Slavery accompanied the birth of the United States and fueled the economy of the South, turning owners into wealthy people while no benefits were garnered by their slaves. Moreover, child labor, mistreatment, families being split apart, and even rape accompanied this racist system.

Slavery and its generational consequences are not the only focus some want minimized or sugar-coated in history books. What about America's indigenous people who were tricked into signing treaties or killed in battle? The stories of the Trail of Tears (Cherokee) and the Long Walk (Navajo) further demonstrate the inhumane treatment Native Americans suffered at the hands of the white majority.

During some of our lifetimes, the United States pulled Japanese-Americans from their families, homes, and workplaces and placed them in internment camps. Over 120,000 citizens were imprisoned this way simply because their Japanese heritage made them suspect during World War II and due to Japan's role of aggressor. Racism perpetuates a disregard for life, turning a person created in God's image into someone to discount and, at times, even deny basic human rights.

And what about in this century? After the deaths of Ahmaud Arbery, Breonna Taylor, George Floyd, and so many others, some thought it was important to remind society that "Black Lives Matter." Others dug in deeply, exploring how systems and structures contribute to racism, arriving with evidence and hypotheses called critical race theory. Wishing to ignore these and so many other needless deaths, many put a target on "Black Lives Matter" and on critical race theory, concluding such efforts are un-Christian and anti-American.

"Black Lives Matter" is an organization but also a slogan, according to the BBC: "Black Lives Matter is a phrase, and notably a hashtag, used to highlight racism, discrimination and inequality experienced by black people. Supporters point to the fact that black people are much more likely to be shot by police in the US."[1]

What's the problem? True, white lives matter, but white folks are not likely to be shot by the police with the same degree of probability as black folks. True, all lives matter to God, but one can only imagine our Heavenly Father's anguish when a subset of his crown of creation is gunned down. Life is sacred, and we need to be so reminded, particularly for our black brothers and sisters.

One of the best explanations of critical race theory is this definition provided by PBS:

> Critical race theory is a way of thinking about America's history through the lens of racism. It centers on the idea that racism is systemic in the nation's institutions and that they function to maintain the dominance of white people in society.[2]

Back to our opening chapter: one way we understand the world around us is by making and testing hypotheses; in this way God reveals what we need to know. If your God is so small that you only focus on individual sin and salvation, then it's time to go back to Genesis and understand that God is the Creator of all. Fields of study such as sociology are tools of general revelation that help us understand interactions of humans and structures such as societies, governments, and other institutions. If you doubt critical race theory, derive your own theory of systems that have operated throughout history—a history that has repeatedly diminished the role of some and empowered the role of others. Until such a more convincing theory emerges, I believe critical race theory is plausible and likely explains the past all the way up to the present among various people groups. Moreover, I reject simplistic Christian viewpoints that are "other worldly," looking only at individuals' souls, thereby only focusing on the destination of heaven instead of the current reality of structures and systems of humanity. God

---

1. Campbell, "What Is Black Lives Matter," paras. 2 and 4.
2. Anderson, "Critical Race Theory," paras. 5–6.

Racism: A Sin That Diminishes Life

created the world, instructed us to care for it—not just limiting us to the material realm—and loved the world so much that God sent his Son, promising that someday the old will pass away and this earth will be restored with "streets of gold."

The human body is a structure with various systems (skeletal, muscular, nervous, endocrine, cardiovascular, lymphatic, respiratory, digestive, urinary, and reproductive); through God's general revelation, we have come to better and better understand these systems and how they work individually and interdependently. Moreover, we have learned to hypothesize about the reason when a system isn't working (i.e., diagnosis) and intervene with treatment (surgery, pharmacology, therapy, etc.). The same is true of human interactions. There are structures that hold society together and within these structures are systems: economic, familial, governmental, and the like. And when one people group seemingly is disadvantaged, the system or systems at fault need to be diagnosed, and we all bear a responsibility to intervene.

Let's go back to the story of our two sons in high school. Truly individual racism was evidenced. However, there was a system in play in which the AD could bench two players without explaining the situation to the coach. The AD was part of a system and exercised his power over a Hispanic coach and two African young men. Yes, individual racism, but also systemic racism.

It is helpful, however, to look at overarching examples of systemic racism to best understand it. The G.I. Bill "was originally called the Servicemen's Readjustment Act and was enacted by the Department of Labor before WWII ended. With the war ending, the US government anticipated around 15 million returning military personnel that would be unemployed. To avoid a post-war depression, the bill provided affordable low-cost mortgages, low tuition, low-interest business loans, unemployment compensation, and tuition assistance."[3] If you are Caucasian, like me, you may be able to look back one, two, or three generations and identify your ancestors who greatly benefited from the G.I. Bill. However, if you are a person of color, finding G.I. Bill beneficiaries on your

---

3. Nowakowski and Larry, "GI Bill," para. 4.

family tree is nearly impossible. Why? Because of the actions of one Southern segregationist congressman, the provision ended up being administered by each state, not the federal government. The results?

> Often, Black veterans were discouraged from applying for the GI Bill and were attacked by racist bystanders with rocks while on their way to federal buildings. Postmasters would also not deliver mail containing necessary paperwork to Black veterans. The Jim Crow "separate but equal" laws impacted the quality of education Black veterans received at universities and trade schools. Black institutions were regularly not as well staffed, trained or equipped to educate their students compared to their white counterparts, with fully equipped supplies. Housing options were also unequal for Black veterans, with valuable homes restricted in the South and redlining forcing Black veterans into depreciating areas in the North.[4]

Perhaps you're unfamiliar with redlining, another facet of systemic racism. Consider this explanation provided by Terry Gross in one of her *Fresh Air* reports:

> The Federal Housing Administration, which was established in 1934, furthered the segregation efforts by refusing to insure mortgages in and near African-American neighborhoods—a policy known as "redlining." At the same time, the FHA was subsidizing builders who were mass-producing entire subdivisions for whites—with the requirement that none of the homes be sold to African-Americans. [As a result] today African-American incomes on average are about 60 percent of average white incomes. But African-American wealth is about 5 percent of white wealth. Most middle-class families in this country gain their wealth from the equity they have in their homes. So this enormous difference between a 60 percent income ratio and a 5 percent wealth ratio is almost entirely attributable to federal housing policy implemented through the 20th century.[5]

4. Nowakowski and Larry, "GI Bill," para. 7.
5. Gross, "'Forgotten History,'" paras. 3 and 11.

Racism: A Sin That Diminishes Life

I want my grandchildren to profit from God's general revelation by a means of analysis—critical race theory—so that they can be faithful Christians, link arms with others, and intervene in such a way that historically disadvantaged groups can flourish not just today, but for years to come.

Some of those who turn a deaf ear to the "Black Lives Matter" slogan seek to ensure universities may not include personnel who work for diversity, equity, and inclusion, and work furiously to make sure critical race theory isn't addressed in schools. For some, this can be setting out on the road to Christian nationalism—a sad case of racism mixed with misguided faith.

Paul Miller, writing in *Christianity Today*, explains Christian nationalism in two steps:

> Most scholars agree that nationalism starts with the belief that humanity is divisible into mutually distinct, internally coherent cultural groups defined by shared traits like language, religion, ethnicity, or culture. From there, scholars say, nationalists believe that these groups should each have their own governments; that governments should promote and protect a nation's cultural identity; and that sovereign national groups provide meaning and purpose for human beings.
>
> Christian nationalism is the belief that the American nation is defined by Christianity, and that the government should take active steps to keep it that way. Popularly, Christian nationalists assert that America is and must remain a "Christian nation"—not merely as an observation about American history, but as a prescriptive program for what America must continue to be in the future. Scholars like Samuel Huntington have made a similar argument: that America is defined by its "Anglo-Protestant" past and that we will lose our identity and our freedom if we do not preserve our cultural inheritance.[6]

Miller goes on and draws out some of the implications: "Christian nationalists do not reject the First Amendment and do not advocate for theocracy, but they do believe that Christianity

---

6. Miller, "What Is Christian Nationalism?," paras. 4–5.

should enjoy a privileged position in the public square." In addition, he notes that "Christian nationalists want to define America as a Christian nation and they want the government to promote a specific cultural template as the official culture of the country."[7]

Do you see the clear desire for homogeneity? White and Christian (and for some, Protestant). This leaves little room for the New Testament new reality: "There is neither Jew nor Gentile, neither slave nor free, nor is there male and female, for you are all one in Christ Jesus" (Gal 3:28). Clearly our Scripture-based goal is to break down walls that separate people and gather them together in oneness in Christ. In addition, pay attention to the picture of the future drawn for us in Rev 7:9: "After this I looked, and there before me was a great multitude that no one could count, from every nation, tribe, people and language, standing before the throne and before the Lamb. They were wearing white robes and were holding palm branches in their hands."

Sometimes these non-biblical efforts are disguised or mostly hidden so that we only see a tip of the iceberg. For instance, is building a wall at the country's southern border simply an attempt to bring more order to the deluge of those seeking to come to America? Or is it a way to promote or protect a more pure Anglo-Protestant America? Are the attempts of state legislators to prohibit critical race theory in schools a way to protect and enshrine a certain cultural template and keep it from losing its influence and power? Is a ban on travel to the US from Muslim countries a matter of national security or a way to safeguard (diminishing) Christianity in the US population? Be careful, for if you peel away the layers of the onion, you may just find a smelly Christian nationalistic effort at the core.

Moreover, if we dig deep, we will often unearth underlying anxiety and dread. So much of racism is fueled by fear. Fear of the other. Fear of losing one's advantage or privilege. Fear of the unknown. Do you really know your hidden thoughts and fears? There are things we do of which we are unaware. Consider microaggressions—often just a few thinly veiled words that slight or put

7. Miller, "What Is Christian Nationalism?," paras. 6 and 9.

down others, intentionally or unintentionally, that reflect insensitivity at best and racism (or other isms) at worst on the speaker's part. For example, when confronted with the unexpected, it would be far better to say a person or something is *going rogue*, instead of saying *going off the reservation*, given the complicated and dismal history associated with American history and Indigenous peoples. I was once in a meeting where a colleague used the phrase, and the Native American member of the group ever so kindly stopped the meeting and explained how that phrase was offensive to her.

Maybe you need a good friend—of a different ethnic group—who can tell you something you can't see clearly about yourself. Perhaps your pastor can hold up a mirror so you can see yourself better. Or consider a good counselor who can help you discover the fears that are keeping you in the chains of racism. Moreover, find your inspiration for change from Scripture.

Fear of the other? "Love the Lord your God with all your heart and with all your soul and with all your mind and with all your strength.' The second is this: 'Love your neighbor as yourself.' There is no commandment greater than these" (Mark 12:30–31). "He executes justice for the fatherless and the widow, and loves the sojourner, giving him food and clothing. Love the sojourner, therefore, for you were sojourners in the land of Egypt" (Deut 10:18–19).

Fear of losing advantage or privilege? "Do not store up for yourselves treasures on earth, where moths and vermin destroy, and where thieves break in and steal. But store up for yourselves treasures in heaven, where moths and vermin do not destroy, and where thieves do not break in and steal. For where your treasure is, there your heart will be also" (Matt 6:19–21). "Blessed are the meek, for they will inherit the earth" (Matt 5:5).

Fear of the unknown? "Do not be anxious about anything, but in every situation, by prayer and petition, with thanksgiving, present your requests to God. And the peace of God, which transcends all understanding, will guard your hearts and your minds in Christ Jesus" (Phil 4:6–7). "Peace I leave with you; my peace I give you. I do not give to you as the world gives. Do not let your hearts be troubled and do not be afraid" (John 14:27).

My hypothesis is that many of us—myself included—really don't know how deeply we have buried a handful or bushel-basket full of racist attitudes. I recall a few decades back when Calvin College (now Calvin University) invited Charles Murray, one of the authors of *The Bell Curve*, to speak on campus; it was disheartening to hear people jump on board and quickly affirm the authors' contention that African-Americans were less intelligent, telling their own stories that sought to confirm the assertion. Of course, most hadn't read the book, nor realized that nearly all of the comparative data was based on highly invalid and unreliable group IQ tests—making it, in my judgment, pseudo-science, not worthy of understanding it as part of God's general revelation.

In addition, we certainly don't understand the extent of our motives or experiences behind these attitudes or how right-wing propaganda sparks these buried feelings. Then, to make matters worse, we live in a society with systems and structures that make it difficult for some and easy for others. On top of this all, some of today's heroes implicitly or explicitly model racism in their words and behaviors, denying any theory of systemic racism.

For example, Elon Musk is an incredibly wealthy, self-made man—a hero to some, living the American dream. But we forget that the first seventeen years of his life were in South Africa and during the apartheid period—a period of systemic racism around which the entire society was built. Should we wonder, then, why, in an interview with Don Lemon, these ideas surfaced:

> In response to questions about his resistance to diversity, equity and inclusion policies (which Musk has decried as racist), Musk argued that the country should "move on" and not make racism "a constant subject." Of late, Musk has been retweeting posts that promote misinformation about the intelligence of racial minorities, Mother Jones has reported. "We are all descended from slaves," Musk said during the interview with Lemon. "Well, not everyone was a slave," Lemon corrected, adding that it was "insulting" for Musk to suggest that people who

experienced racism or discrimination should "just move forward and ignore the past."[8]

The mention of *Mother Jones* refers to an article they published—with a video—that explains how certain platforms on X (formerly Twitter) return to the theme that black people are innately intellectually inferior; Musk then endorses them, and his endorsement furthers the play such posts get. The *Mother Jones* article makes this point:

> Because this racism is seemingly backed by scientific fact, people often lack the language to call out its problematic nature. "There's a kind of fusion between old-school gutter racism that everyone can recognize and this new-school Silicon Valley, data-driven analysis. And I think that this is very confusing to people," said Gusev [a statistical geneticist from Harvard Medical School]. "They don't know what to do with it. They say, 'Hey, there's this thing that I recognize as ugly, and then there's somebody posting a hundred charts that seem to support it.'"[9]

A marriage of pseudo-science (as was also the case with *The Bell Curve*) and slick Silicon Valley marketing—all to further Musk's profits, and also unmasking his own racism.

If we wish to rid ourselves of racist attitudes and start to see the obstacles in society and in the institutions in which we find ourselves, we must develop ways to see injustice and root it out. For while fear may be the personal stumbling block for individuals, injustice is the companion boulder that fuels systemic racism.

What does the Lord require? Micah 6:8 says, "He has shown you, O mortal, what is good. And what does the Lord require of you? To act justly and to love mercy and to walk humbly with your God."

Martin Luther King Jr. explained the difference between just laws and unjust laws: "A just law is a man-made code that squares

---

8. Telford, "Five Key Moments," paras. 19–21.
9. Coghill and Hayes, "Elon Musk Keeps Spreading," paras. 6–7.

with the moral law or the law of God. An unjust law is a code that is out of harmony with the moral law."[10] He goes on and provides a structural analysis:

> An unjust law is a code that a numerical or power majority group compels a minority group to obey but does not make binding on itself. This is *difference* made legal. By the same token, a just law is a code that a majority compels a minority to follow and that it is willing to follow itself. This is *sameness* made legal.[11]

While one should debate whether the goal should still be sameness, as this illustration shows, the historical context in which King wrote was one of *differences* made legal: separate drinking fountains, separate seating on buses, and the like.

FIGURE 4[12]

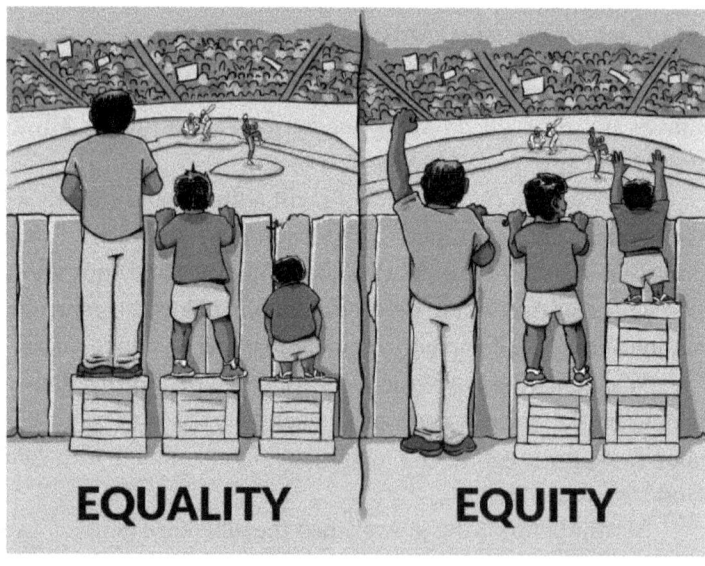

10. King, *Why We Can't Wait*, 70.
11. King, *Why We Can't Wait*, 71.
12. Illustration from the Interaction Institute for Social Change, artist Angus Maguire.

Racism: A Sin That Diminishes Life

But lest you believe that the civil rights years made such a focus no longer necessary, please know that there are still laws that are being maintained or added, for example, that put up obstacles for people of color to vote, that gerrymander districts to ensure the impact of people of color is dissipated in elections, and that increase schools' dependence on property taxes.

Theologian Howard Thurman uncovered the role of power in the perpetuation of racism in our society:

> The threat of violence within a framework of well-high limitedness power is a weapon by which the weak are held in check. Artificial limitations are placed upon them, restricting freedom of movement, of employment, and of participation in the common life. These limitations are given formal or informal expression in general or specific policies of separateness or segregation. These policies tend to freeze the social status of the insecure. The threat of violence may be implemented not only by constituted authority but also by anyone acting in behalf of the established order. Every member of the controllers' group is in a sense a special deputy, authorized by the mores to enforce the pattern.[13]

Oh, you say, this is no longer the case. Really? "Artificial limitations are placed upon them, restricting freedom of movement." Why did that police car follow our son through the lily white suburb? Perhaps it wasn't a limitation, but it sure gave a message about whether our son was welcome to drive and move through that suburb. "The threat of violence may be implemented . . . by anyone acting in behalf of the established order." Does the name of Kyle Rittenhouse come to mind?[14] Mr. Rittenhouse had an AR-15-style rifle that he brought to a protest in Kenosha, Wisconsin—a protest in response to a white police officer having shot an African-American man. The result? Mr. Rittenhouse shot and killed two people. While he was acquitted because the jury concluded he acted in

---

13. Thurman, *Jesus and the Disinherited*, 31.
14. Sullivan, "Kyle Rittenhouse Is Acquitted," paras. 1–7.

self-defense, this was a young man who was a resident of Illinois and had gone to this rally with a gun—a self-appointed vigilante.

Christian leader John Perkins tells the story of his arrest and trial in one of his early books. In telling this story, he reminds us both of systemic racism and our role:

> Whether we admit it or not, our reading of biblical ethics is colored by our perception of the world around us. If we think that there are only a few "bad guys" such as burglars and murderers, and that all the given political, legal and economic structures around us are basically okay, then we are bound to read our Bibles in a certain way. But that assumption can be badly shaken up by a good look at what happens to many people who are simply crushed by, rather than helped by, these social structures and institutions we take for granted. If sin can exist at every level of government, and in every human institution, then also the call to biblical justice in every corner of society must be sounded by those who claim a God of Justice as their Lord.[15]

Yes, we must sound the trumpet to call out injustice that is built upon racism or any other life-denying attitude or practice. While some contend that once America had elected its first black president, we moved to a post-racial society, this belief is naïve. As Perkins points out, sin exists at every level of government and in every human institution. An election simply doesn't root out sin that quickly or comprehensively.

In addition, this call is not only to individuals; the church must be vocal as well. Unfortunately, the criticism Martin Luther King Jr. leveled at the church is seemingly more true today than when he wrote from the Birmingham jail: "So often the contemporary church is a weak, ineffectual voice with an uncertain sound. . . . If today's church does not recapture the sacrificial spirt of the early church, it will lose its authenticity, forfeit the loyalty of millions, and be dismissed as an irrelevant social club with no meaning for the 20th century. Every day I meet young people

---

15. Perkins, *Let Justice Roll Down*, 195.

RACISM: A SIN THAT DIMINISHES LIFE

whose disappointment with the church has turned into outright disgust."[16]

When discussing current events with or without the possibility of appealing to Scripture, I hope you will demonstrate your advocacy for life—for the flourishing of life for all. Remember this quote from Martin Luther King Jr.: "Injustice anywhere is a threat to justice everywhere."[17]

If some cannot be convinced of individual and systemic racism, lead them to the broad implications of tolerating injustice. In the soccer story earlier in this chapter, the implication of benching our sons was an injustice to other members of the team as well: they lost their two teammates who were the two leading scorers of the team. Working or going to school in a lily white environment deprives people of learning how to work with others, both appreciating their culture and their contributions. Attending a lily white church deprives those in the front and those in the pew of the rich spiritual legacy of African-Americans, as their songs and perspectives are missed much of the time (except, perhaps, during Black History Month!).

WHAT YOU CAN DO TO PROMOTE LIFE

Discussing racism is fraught with challenges. Defensiveness quickly sets in and listening shuts down. Yet, in matters of race, injustice, and discrimination, we need to promote life. I love to rely on Rev 7, conveying in words the picture of God gathering to himself those from every nation, tribe, people and language. Telling a story—a personal story if possible—is one way to open up this picture to discussion. While our son Paul was in the hospital for a month, our daughter Jessica drew this picture for him—and it hung in his hospital room those many weeks. Better than words, it became Paul's witness to all who entered his room.

16. King, *Why We Can't Wait*, 80.
17. King, *Why We Can't Wait*, 65.

FIGURE 5

8

Criminal Justice and Incarceration: Life Locked Up

WHY WOULD A CHAPTER about criminal justice and punishment be in a book about promoting life? Consider Matt 25:35–40:

> "For I was hungry and you gave me something to eat, I was thirsty and you gave me something to drink, I was a stranger and you invited me in, I needed clothes and you clothed me, I was sick and you looked after me, I was in prison and you came to visit me." Then the righteous will answer him, "Lord, when did we see you hungry and feed you, or thirsty and give you something to drink? When did we see you a stranger and invite you in, or needing clothes and clothe you? When did we see you sick or in prison and go to visit you?" The King will reply, "Truly I tell you, whatever you did for one of the least of these brothers and sisters of mine, you did for me."

Notice that care for those in prison is listed along addressing the needs of those who are hungry, thirsty, needing clothing, and sick. These are all, prison as well, conditions that rob us and others from life. And in this text, Jesus wants us to know, as he addresses the topic of eternal life, that our lives are to be lived with care and compassion in response to his saving love. Promoting life, even to those we tend to forget in prison.

For a short while, I was able to preach in a prison worship service. Truly, each service was moving and Spirit-filled, for many of the prisoners found this time to be freeing (of course, there were always a few that used it as a chance to deviate from their daily routine and spread whatever deviance they could during the service). I recall one young man who came up to me after the service. He shared with me that he grew up in various locations around the world, since his father was in the military. He told me of his accomplishments, but said not a word about why he was serving time. Why? He wanted to make sure I saw him as fully a person, not just a prisoner, someone who had been robbed of his identity.

This young man was undoubtedly in prison for a valid reason, and imprisonment was the result of our justice system. Let's look a bit at our justice system and the corresponding level of imprisonment in the United States. We will do so by leaning on the work of the World Justice Project, an international group committed to the rule of law and with people like James Baker (former U.S. Secretary of State), Stephen Beyer (former U.S. Supreme Court justice) and former President Jimmy Carter lending their names to the effort.[1]

Their foundational position is one that certainly flows from the Judeo-Christian tradition even with leadership in the group from Muslim and other traditions: "An effective criminal justice system is an essential component of the rule of law, as it functions to reduce crime and provide reparations for victims. In particular, the procedural apparatus of a criminal justice system that upholds the rule of law must be fair, impartial, and respectful of the human rights of those involved—for both victims and for the accused."[2]

While this report is a handful of years old, I suspect the trend they presented—a decrease in factors such as protecting the rights of the victims and the accused and timeliness—continues in the areas they cited, with a focus on East Asia, Europe, and North America (primarily the United States). They share a response of a European leader who reflects on their data:

---

1. World Justice Project, "What the Data Says," para. 1.
2. World Justice Project, "What the Data Says," para. 2.

> Christopher Lehman, Executive Director of the CEELI Institute, points out, "populism is currently disrupting criminal justice systems in Europe, specifically within the central and eastern European region. Governments increasingly demonize the judiciary and this external pressure interferes with judicial independence. In some cases it makes the judiciary less willing to do what is necessary to protect the rights of defendants, to fully ensure access to justice, and it often results in the judiciary's self-censoring."[3]

The CEELI institute is headquartered in the Czech Republic, so it is no surprise that its magnifying glass is fixed on Europe. Yet, there are aspects of Mr. Lehman's statement about the threat populism brings which could be applied to certain trends in the United States, particularly the demonization of the judiciary. A more recent report from the World Justice Project confirms that trend:

> Since 2016, [the United States] has dropped four places in the Index ranking, and its score is down 5% overall. We have seen a particularly sharp drop in the U.S. score for "constraints on government powers"—down 15% since 2016, with a 16% decline in the sub-factor measuring judicial constraints on executive power; only fifteen countries in the world have seen a sharper decline in this metric over this period. One of the survey questions we ask is whether people think a high government official who commits a crime will be held accountable; when we asked that question in 2014, 60% considered the official likely to be held accountable; in 2021, it had dropped to 24%.[4]

Certainly, we must insist on both the rights of victims and those accused—from high government officials to those on the margins and all in between—while rebuffing populism and insisting on the rule of law. It's the best and only way to recognize the crown of

---

3. World Justice Project, "What the Data Says," para. 11.
4. World Justice Project, "Democracy's Last Line of Defense," para. 7.

God's creation and our complicity in our first parents' failure to abide by God's rule for them.

Another important international comparison relates to one of the frequent outcomes of our justice system: incarceration. According to the Prison Policy Initiative, "not only does the U.S. have the highest incarceration rate in the world; every single U.S. state incarcerates more people per capita than virtually any independent democracy on earth."[5] Moreover, the National Institute for Corrections suggests the findings of a study group that "the U.S. prison population is largely drawn from the most disadvantaged part of the nation's population: mostly men under age 40, disproportionately minority, and poorly educated. Prisoners often carry additional deficits of drug and alcohol addictions, mental and physical illnesses, and lack of work preparation or experience."[6] These data should lead us to immediately ask "Why?"

That same study group came to this conclusion: "The unprecedented rise in incarceration rates can be attributed to an increasingly punitive political climate surrounding criminal justice policy formed in a period of rising crime and rapid social change. This provided the context for a series of policy choices—across all branches and levels of government—that significantly increased sentence lengths, required prison time for minor offenses, and intensified punishment for drug crimes." The authors go on to conclude, from their review of the research, that "the change in penal policy over the past four decades may have had a wide range of unwanted social costs, and the magnitude of crime reduction benefits is highly uncertain."[7]

What might those social costs be? These authors note the impact on prisons and prisoners includes greater overcrowding, increases in mental health problems and suicides, and less and less opportunity for health care and rehabilitative programming. After prison, the authors find greater joblessness, family breakdown,

---

5. Prison Policy Initiative, "States of Incarceration," 2.
6. Travis et al., "Growth of Incarceration," 4.
7. Travis et al, "Growth of Incarceration," 7.

violence, and substance abuse among those re-entering society, but admit that these increases in incarceration cause such outcomes. So the obvious question is why are we incarcerating at a rate so much higher than the rest of the world, particularly when this increase has not led to greater success? My hypothesis—as in other issues of dehumanizing segments of our population—is fear. Unconcerned about rising societal financial costs, discouraging outcomes, and disproportioned rates among minorities, I believe many Americans would rather have people put away, remain out of sight, and stuck behind bars than address root causes and seek true rehabilitation. Simply stated, the cry is "Lock them up!"

But we claim to be fully for life, there is much we can do, and much has already begun out of faith communities. Apart from political action by groups, take note of promising efforts within prisons and after release.

In my "neighborhood," both Calvin University and Hope College have educational degree programs for those in Ionia and Muskegon prisons. Also, those same prisons hold worship services and, in one, a church has organized. Truly, along with countless programs of tutoring, adult education classes, and just plain visiting, those in prison receive hope and skills and, ideally, experience a change of culture within the prison. Consider the testimony of one inmate at the Richard A. Handlon Correctional Facility (often referred to as MTU) in Ionia, Michigan—one who has graduated with his degree from the Calvin Prison Initiative (CPI) and stepped into a mentoring role:

> As a peer-to-peer mentor, I've helped people learn how to read, helped them obtain their GEDs and met some extraordinary people. I know my involvement as mentor has helped others, but it has also deeply affected me. I have been incarcerated for 16 years now, and in all that time I have never felt more fulfilled. In helping other men, I have found my purpose and calling. I have found peace in this chaotic place....
>
> Showing genuine kindness in prison without ulterior motives or the prospect of attachment may not be considered normal, but the mentors at MTU have shed

the chains of institutionalization, exemplifying how a convict has the power to rise above his/her worst choice. Ultimately, the goal of all CPI graduates is to be an agent of renewal within the prison system; therefore, it is imperative that mentors continue to break the norms of prisoner behavior—shifting from convict to mentor—while changing the culture around them and within themselves.[8]

The paragraph that introduces Mr. Horton's words notes a hypothesis that could be realized across the country: "The hope and goal of those who created the CPI program—professors from Calvin College and Calvin Theological Seminary—is to change the violent nature often found within prisons by offering a quality education. The idea was premised on the fact that educated people are less likely to reoffend, and yes, the violence at MTU has dropped significantly since the inception of the CPI program."[9] "I was in prison and you came to visit me."

Opportunities to step more fully into the lives of prisoners expand greatly upon their release. These re-entering citizens have so many challenges, particularly when considering the obstacles cited above (substance abuse, family breakdown, violence, and joblessness). If these and other obstacles are to be avoided and flourishing regained, consider these three areas of opportunity.

First, restorative justice efforts can be found in many communities. Such efforts, depending on the willingness of both victim and offender, open the door to mercy, healing, and restoration—so needed by both parties and, in the case of the offender, the way to experience still another way for release from the chains of past behavior and patterns and for transformation toward a new identity worthy of their Creator.

Second, those re-entering society need to find community. Often, their communities of the past are not accessible to them due to fractured relationships or should be avoided given the depths of drug abuse, violence, and crime embedded within them. Thus,

8. Horton, "From Convict to Mentor," paras 8, 18.
9. Horton, "From Convict to Mentor," para. 1.

we should open the doorways to new communities, and one of the best communities I can think of is the local church. Less than a block away from our church is a re-entry home for those formerly imprisoned due to sexual offenses. Seriously? Yes, a community of belief should have arms open wide enough to embrace such individuals and practices that are protective both for these former offenders and the congregants. We have safe-church policies in place that include their membership in households that do not include children, with after-church policies of monitoring the halls and classrooms, and insistence on a mentor. The result? For many, First Christian Reformed Church is an initial, albeit temporary, worshiping community for those re-entering; for others, they have become members and even stepped into roles of leadership such as the deaconate.

Finally, for those coming out of prison, employment is key. Some companies in my "neighborhood" have opened their doors to ex-offenders, making special efforts to provide employment. As I pen these words, the unemployment is low, so employers are looking beyond their usual horizons for workers. Of course, with employment comes the need for communities to assist with transportation and perhaps a new wardrobe! In addition, in many places, correctional facilities are doubling their efforts on providing job training while in prison. One such effort in Michigan includes "vocational villages" formed in prison; recently they reported that of 1,641 people who had completed the program, 72 percent found jobs while released on parole.[10] Compare that to a report by the Prison Policy Initiative on joblessness: "A good guess [of unemployment] would be 60%, to generalize from a new report released by the Bureau of Justice Statistics. The report shows that of more than 50,000 people released from federal prisons in 2010, a staggering 33% found no employment at all over four years post-release, and at any given time, no more than 40% of the cohort was employed."[11]

---

10. Li, "Tight Labor Market," para. 25.

11. Wang and Bertram, "New Data on Formerly Incarcerated," para. 1.

Never been inside a prison? It's time to make a visit—plan ahead by understanding the policies and steps needed. Ignore the sometimes brusque words and attitudes from the guards; they're just doing their jobs. Experience a little bit of vulnerability by leaving your purse/wallet, car keys, and phone behind and submitting yourself to a head-to-toe search. It's time to set aside your fears and know that each prisoner is fearfully and wonderfully made! As Christ's teachings forcibly show, find a prison in your neighborhood!

WHAT YOU CAN DO TO PROMOTE LIFE

As each chapter ends with this charge, I've often provided suggestions for a conversational context—with a friend, a fellow pew-sitter, or the like. But in this case, I have a different suggestion. Assuming most readers haven't entered a prison, now is the time! Whether a county jail or a state prison, it's time to experience what being in prison means. Check out local ministries, and I'm sure you'll find one that will allow you to slip in. While the experience will not lend itself to understand what incarcerated life involves, it will give you a taste—and, hopefully, convince you to uphold the sanctity of life among those currently or formerly imprisoned.

9

Welcoming the Sojourner: Living with Open Hearts

ON MY FACEBOOK FEED one morning I saw this message in bold: "Don't forget to pay your taxes by April 15 because 30+ million illegal aliens are depending on you." When something on Facebook causes my temperature to rise, I do two things. First, I search for the truth. In this instance, I turned to the Pew Research Center: "The U.S. unauthorized immigrant population rose rapidly from 1990 to 2007 before declining sharply for two years and stabilizing at 10.5 million in 2017."[1] "The unauthorized immigrant population in the United States reached 10.5 million in 2021, according to new Pew Research Center estimates. That was a modest increase over 2019 but nearly identical to 2017."[2] So, the Facebook statement, with a gross exaggeration of the number of unauthorized immigrants in the US, tried to trigger my anger, especially by suggesting my taxes paid for them. While it may be the case that some of my taxes pay for their schooling, there is very little else:

> Are undocumented immigrants eligible for federal public benefit programs? Generally no. Undocumented immigrants, including DACA holders, are ineligible to receive most federal public benefits, including means-tested

---

1. Lopez et al., "Key Facts," para. 4.
2. Passel and Krogstad, "What We Know," para. 1.

> benefits such as Supplemental Nutrition Assistance Program (SNAP, sometimes referred to as food stamps), regular Medicaid, Supplemental Security Income (SSI), and Temporary Assistance for Needy Families (TANF). Undocumented immigrants are ineligible for health care subsidies under the Affordable Care Act (ACA) and are prohibited from purchasing unsubsidized health coverage on ACA exchanges.[3]

Two untruths! Designed to trigger in me and many others anger and action—anger at unauthorized immigrants and voting action to vote for politicians voicing the same false claims.

The second thing I do? I try to withhold my response, afraid that some of my anger—often in the form of sarcasm—will slip in. Nevertheless, we need to be people of the truth.

In this chapter we will look at both immigration and unauthorized immigration, tackling such subjects as the US' southern border, asylum seekers, and DREAMers. Relying on specific revelation, we will begin with Old Testament passages, but first we must understand who the sojourner was. According to the Oxford Bibliographies, this is the meaning:

> This Hebrew term and its translation convey the basic idea that a person (or group) is residing, either temporarily or permanently, in a community and place that is not primarily their own and is dependent on the "goodwill" of that community for their continued existence.[4]

These next passages all refer to the foreigner or sojourner and make it pretty clear that the Israelites of the Old Testament needed to care for them, often reminding them that they, too, were once sojourners.

Exodus 23:9: "Do not oppress a foreigner; you yourselves know how it feels to be foreigners, because you were foreigners in Egypt."

---

3. National Immigration Forum, "Fact Sheet," para. 1.
4. Spencer, "Sojourner," para. 1.

Leviticus 19:33 and 34: "When a foreigner resides among you in your land, do not mistreat them. The foreigner residing among you must be treated as your native-born. Love them as yourself, for you were foreigners in Egypt. I am the Lord your God."

Deuteronomy 10:18–19: "He executes justice for the fatherless and the widow, and loves the sojourner, giving him food and clothing. Love the sojourner, therefore, for you were sojourners in the land of Egypt."

Zechariah 7:10: "Do not oppress the widow, the fatherless, the sojourner, or the poor, and let none of you devise evil against another in your hearts."

Malachi 3:5: "Then I will draw near to you for judgment. I will be a swift witness against the sorcerers, against the adulterers, against those who swear falsely, against those who oppress the hired worker in his wages, the widow and the fatherless, against those who thrust aside the sojourners, and do not fear me, says the Lord of Hosts."

Do Old Testament instructions to the Israelites apply to us? Yes, they do, as the New Testament fulfills the Old Testament pronouncements. In Eph 2:19, the verse refers to the foreigner ("Consequently, you are no longer foreigners and strangers, but fellow citizens with God's people and also members of his household") as Paul made the case that we were no longer Jews or Gentiles, but one in Christ. In other words, the fulfillment of all of the Old Testament texts about sojourners and foreigners is that we are all together now, called by Christ. The bottom line: God insists we care for the sojourner since we are all part of God's humanity.

So how might we, in our pro-life commitments, exercise care for the sojourner in our neighborhood or community? In order to answer this question, we should explore legal immigration before moving to unauthorized immigration.

Our experiences with the sojourners among us began many years ago when we provided transitional living to Louis, a seventeen-year-old who had fled Haiti. He was placed with us by Bethany Christian Services in cooperation with the appropriate federal office. After a number of months where we did our best introducing him to American ways, Louis was on his own. More than thirty years later, he is a productive citizen working in the Grand Rapids metropolitan area.

Through our church, we've also been able to come alongside refugee families. In recent years it has been a Congolese family of four, a Syrian family of four, and most recently, a Congolese family of twelve. These families were displaced from their homes and, upon crossing an international border, became refugees. For the most recent family of twelve, it was more than a twenty-year wait in a refugee camp in Rwanda before they had the opportunity to resettle in the US.

Coming alongside means working with a resettlement agency in the short term and remaining in friendship with the family for the long haul. Transportation to medical appointments, ways to minimize food costs, using public transportation, and developing English skills are just a few of the many things in which we are blessed to be involved.

Recently, my wife, Barb, took the matriarch of the family, Ariada, to the physician's office for an appointment. Barb wondered if she should go into the exam room with Ariada (my wife is a nurse and one of her specialties is women's health), so she asked the translator to ask Ariada if that's what she desired. Through the interpreter, Ariada, mindful that Barb and I are a couple, responded, "Of course, Steve loves us." While I'm not trying to be proud, I was so happy when my wife repeated the story to me. Of course, "we love Steve" would have been fine, but that they experienced my love for them told me I was following the biblical injunction to love neighbor as self.

So how many such refugee families are there each year coming to the US? One source reports that 60,014 refugees were admitted to the US in 2023, an increase from 2022 when the number was 25,465; in 1992 the number surpassed 125,000.[5] From 2010 to 2020 those from Myanmar comprised the greatest number of refugees admitted to the US, followed by those from Iraq and Bhutan. A snapshot taken in 2022, however, shows a different picture, with

---

5. Korhonen, "Number of Refugee Admissions," para. 1.

the greatest number from the Democratic Republic of Congo, then Syria, Myanmar, and Sudan.[6]

Some worry about the process—whether refugees who may potentially resettle here pose some degree of risk. The process, detailed below, suggests the vetting is extraordinary.

> The U.S. State Department, in consultation with a constellation of other agencies and organizations, manages the process through its refugee admission program, US-RAP. The first step for a potential refugee abroad is most often to register with the UN High Commissioner for Refugees (UNHCR). UNHCR officials collect documentation and perform an initial screening and then refer qualifying individuals to State Department Resettlement Support Centers (RSCs), of which there are seven around the world . . . . Then, RSC officials interview the applicants, verify their personal data, and submit their information for background checks by a suite of U.S. national security agencies. These security checks include multiple forms of biometric screening, such as cross-checks of global fingerprint databases and medical tests. If none of these inquiries produce problematic results, including criminal histories, past immigration violations, connections to terrorist groups, or communicable diseases, the applicant can be cleared for entry to the United States.[7]

So, the refugees being admitted to the US provide a wonderful opportunity to promote life—helping a family adjust, find jobs, and begin to succeed economically, educationally, physically, socially, and spiritually are all promoting life. But what about others who come?

Those who come via pathways different from that described above use a variety of means, but key is obtaining permanent immigrant status—often referred to as a "green card"—which allows working in the US and provides a path to citizenship. Five of the most often used ways of obtaining a green card are via a family basis (e.g., marriage), employment (e.g., those in a vocational area

---

6. Klobucista et al., "How Does the U.S.," para. 16.
7. Klobucista et al., "How Does the U.S.," paras. 19–21.

that the US needs), long-time residency (before 1972), the diversity lottery, and humanitarian reasons (e.g., asylum, human trafficking, etc.).

The last two, in particular, may acutely call forth our care for the sojourner. First, the diversity lottery. Each year, fifty thousand individuals are selected at random from countries with low rates of immigration to the US. While socioeconomic status (SES) is not a factor, often those of a lower SES living in a country with little economic opportunity apply. Those folks I know who have "won" the lottery have needed the care and love of the Christian community. Unlike admitted refugees who are able to obtain Medicaid, food stamps, and other forms of assistance early on, diversity lottery winners have no particular support network to enter. Situations I've known are when a winner attends community ESL classes and gets connected to a church community as a result or when the winner finds an Ethiopian community in the US that provides welcome and assistance. Finding housing, transportation, medical care, jobs, and food are immediate challenges.

The fifth pathway, humanitarian reasons, opens up the discussion of our challenges at the US southern border. People from South and Central America can be living in fear for a host of reasons, so many travel to the southern border to seek asylum. News accounts will tell you the system for reviewing the cases is swamped, and while recent policy changes mean the asylum seekers must remain in Mexico while they wait for their appointments, living conditions can be inhumane. Of course, some at the border try to sneak across the border, often at great risk and loss of life.

What is the pro-life response to this situation, particularly when Congress seems to have little appetite to fix the system and would rather decry the situation as a way to complain about the other political party? Loving your neighbor—directly or indirectly—can occur in three locales.

First, while it seems a long shot, improving the conditions in these people's home countries is needed. Living without fear, with necessary resources, and with hope could keep people from fleeing. Check out the Association for a More Just Society,[8] which has labored in Honduras since 1998, decreasing homicides, targeting corruption in the government, and seeking justice in the policing system. Seek to vote for US officials that seemingly understand the complexities of improving situations abroad to lessen the impact at the border.

The second locale is at the border. There are organizations on either side of the border that love their neighbors. Those waiting in desperate conditions are helped by a variety of churches and ministries. In the San Diego-Tijuana area, Baptists on both sides of the border have come together to help these sojourners.[9] Incidentally, fear-mongers tell us we need to build a wall. However, the vast majority (between 78 and 87 percent) of those who seek to cross unlawfully are prevented or apprehended.[10]

Before moving on to the third locale, it is instructive to understand the current process—albeit a process that gets modified from time to time by Executive Order, but changes often get "stayed" or thrown out by the courts. The key relates to seeking asylum. The US law says "an individual qualifies for asylum if they can reach the United States (whether or not at a designated port of arrival) *and* can demonstrate that, if returned, they face a well-founded fear of persecution on account of their race, religion, political opinion, national origin or membership in a particular social group."[11] Thus, "migrants . . . present themselves to U.S. Customs and Border Protection officials at ports of entry and request asylum. Undocumented migrants who are apprehended while trying to cross the border illegally between ports of entry also can request asylum."[12]

Presenting to the U.S. Customs and Border Protection means a stay at a U.S. Customs and Border Protection facility and an interview by an asylum officer. If the migrant passes the interview,

---

8. See www.asj-us.org/.
9. Cockes, "California Baptists in Migrant Ministry," para. 1.
10. Soerens, "Border Is a Mess," para. 6.
11. Soerens, "Border Is a Mess," para. 9.
12. Goldstein and Cai, "What Do Migrants Experience?," para. 3.

then they are entitled to a full court hearing by a judge. While the migrant waits for the full hearing, there are four possible places where that wait may occur: (1) back in Mexico, (2) at an ICE detention center, (3) released from detention, or, (4) for unaccompanied minors, a migrant children's shelter.[13]

Now on to the third locale, particularly for those released from detention (item 3, above) and who must wait for their full court hearing. While at times a sponsor is sought for these individuals and families to stay with, in many cases these asylum seekers are bused or flown, without any preparation beyond disembarking, to cities such as San Antonio; Miramar, Florida; Los Angeles; Jacksonville, Florida; Milwaukee; Chicago; Washington, DC; Denver; New York City; and Mount Laurel, New Jersey. Regardless where they land, the wait can be four to ten years for the court hearing.[14] While they are free to live and work (after an initial waiting period of six months for a work permit) in the US while waiting, most often these cities are not ready for them. So, what should a pro-lifer do? Come alongside them—much like churches and individuals have learned to do for refugees—and help them find housing, assist them in job searching, and offer them love and acceptance. There is no need to be negative or judgmental. These individuals are well within the law and are living in limbo. Are their hopes realistic? Various reports tell us that just 20 percent[15] to 40 percent are granted asylum; those failing to get asylum are deported.[16]

One last matter to consider: DREAMers (Development, Relief and Education for Alien Minors). During the Obama administration, about five hundred thousand young people who were brought illegally by parents into the US or whose parents had their visas expire were given protection as young people via the Deferred Action for Childhood Arrivals (DACA). This program gave them the ability to work and continue their schooling and kept them from being deported. Subsequent administrations tried to kill the

---

13. Goldstein and Cai, "What Do Migrants Experience?," paras. 5, 8–9.
14. Spagat, "Immigrants Waiting 10 Years," para. 6.
15. Valverde, "False Claim That 80%," para. 9.
16. Soerens, "Border Is a Mess," para. 15.

Welcoming the Sojourner: Living with Open Hearts

program, and it has been tied up in the courts while an additional 1.1 million young people wait to be included.[17] At the time of this writing, it seems that they've been altogether forgotten.

Imagine being ready to move into adulthood with dreams shaped by growing up in the US, dreams of living where one desires, working at a job with a decent income, and having a family. Yet, you need to live under the radar—you can't get federal aid for higher education, you aren't allowed to work. Why? Because of something your parents did when you were two or three: they let their visas expire or they entered the US illegally. This equates to being punished for their parents' sins of commission or omission.

What does it mean to be pro-life? Insist that this young person go back to a country that they don't know—perhaps even a language they can't speak? In my opinion, that's not pro-life; that's pro-legalism. What does the New Testament tell us? Christ came to fulfill the law and we are to live by loving God and our neighbors as ourselves. In this instance, love should propel us to advocate for these young people whether it be in our voting, in our letter writing, or in our conversations. Back to all of the words from the Old Testament, for truly these young people are defenseless sojourners: "love them as yourself," "giving him food and clothing," and never are they to be "thrust aside."

As I reflect on my experiences with refugees and DREAMers, I have always been struck by the ways in which these friends are desirous of being contributing members of American society. While I didn't know my ancestors who immigrated to America three or four generations before me, arriving via Ellis Island, I suspect the similarities between them and today's newcomers are many: helped by churches and those of similar ethnicities, eager to work—even at the most menial jobs—and believing that America would be the best of all possible options for their families. I'd like to think the torch of the Statue of Liberty still shines, welcoming all with these words inscribed on the pedestal: "Give me your tired, your poor, your huddled masses yearning to breathe free."

---

17. Gamboa, "No Allies Left," para. 4.

WHAT YOU CAN DO TO PROMOTE LIFE

Is the system broken? For displaced persons waiting in a refugee camp, some might criticize the system. However, I maintain the system works—including the diversity lottery—but waits are long, and the capacity for such immigrants is limited. In contrast to the system for those waiting their turn in refugee camps, the system used for those fleeing to the United States to enter at the southern border is flawed—something admitted by both political parties to varying degrees. As you read the earlier pages, I suspect you wondered why the initial asylum review allows many to advance to multiple year waits only to be denied asylum. Does the system unwittingly allow people to slide out of the waiting period and simply live in an undocumented status? Are too many allowed to stay for a much later asylum hearing if the outcomes for so many are negative? Inasmuch as you engage the political process, it is fairly simple to see that we need to invest more into building the review system, for our immigration system of judges and courts is inadequate to deal with the numbers of people the system needs to handle.

We can look at systems dispassionately, but stories trigger our emotions. Recently, an undocumented DREAMer killed his girlfriend in our community—truly a horrible act. Quickly, one of the candidates for president appeared in our town, decrying the problem and claiming he had the solution. Best to go beyond politics.

Consider what one church did as reported by a local news outlet. One Saturday evening, a church member found this young man in the church. He called the pastor, and she suggested a place be made in the building for him to spend the night. Just as importantly, the pastor went to the church to talk with this stranger and pray with him.

> "He was just having a really bad time. He had lost his job, he'd been in a fight, been kicked out of where he lived, so he was basically kind of homeless," she said he told her. "He never told me exactly what was bothering him, but I knew he was very upset. He got very emotional while we were talking, crying to the point where I gave him

Kleenex." He told her he had family in Grand Rapids, but that they wouldn't have him. "'I've disappointed them too many times. They aren't going to,'" she recalled him saying.[18]

The next morning was Palm Sunday, and the young man came to worship, but during the service, he slipped out, went to the church basement, and used the phone to turn himself in.

My point is this. Whether in conversations about undocumented immigrants or should we meet up with one, the correct posture, as shown by this pastor and her church, is one of mercy. The vast majority of us are not running for political office, nor are we charged with policy creation or enforcement. Rather, we are called to promote life by showing mercy and to trust justice will be done.

---

18. Kolker, "Ruby Garcia Murder Suspect," paras 11–14.

10

The Struggle for Life in War Zones

AUTHOR JOEL RICHARDSON WAS preaching at a nearby megachurch. So, when the sermon was posted online, I watched and listened. This is how he began, responding to the Hamas attack on Israel of October 7, 2023:

> When I see other humans attacked for no other reason other than the fact they are Jewish, being raped, kidnapped, killed, murdered, I'm going to stand with them, stand with them. I don't care if they are Jewish, Muslim, Hindu, whatever. I'm a human and we need to stand with people when they are oppressed. This is what the God of heaven does. He stands with the needy, the afflicted, the forgotten, the rejected, the hated, the marginalized; the gospel is for the poor.

As much as I could affirm this opening perspective and the way in which he seemingly valued the lives of all, he then reached into Joel 3:1–3 and made the case that the scattering of God's people, of their being taken into captivity, and their land being divided up had not only happened in history, but the events of October 7 gave evidence of a contemporary effort with the same goal. Therefore, he instructed the congregation, saying, "Standing in solidarity with Israel and the global Jewish community—it is one of the most important calls on the people of God, the church today is to stand with them—those the whole world is turning against."

The Struggle for Life in War Zones

He went on, suggesting that to take the side of the Palestinians in any way was the result of brainwashing:

> After October 7 [2023] Israel was invaded—over 1200 plus people were murdered, a couple hundred people were kidnapped—taken prisoners of war. . . . the nations joined them [Hamas or Palestinians—the pronoun is unclear in its reference] in the streets, celebrating including many western kids—all of our kids being brainwashed at universities—I'm not saying don't send your kids to college but there's obviously a lot of indoctrination there and they think they are joining the justice issue of the day.[1]

Hmmm. This sermon was delivered on February 4, 2024. Truly, the actions of Hamas toward the nation of Israel and her people were pure evil. But on February 4, 2024, not only had "1200 plus" Israelis been murdered four months earlier, as he said, but as of February 4, 2024, the date of Richardson's sermon, the report from the Palestinian Ministry of Health said "at least 27,365 people have been killed and 66,630 injured in Gaza since the October 7 Hamas attacks and Israel's ensuing offensive in the enclave."[2] (Five months later, in early July, the number of deaths climbed to 38,000, with 70 percent being women and children.)[3]

Moreover, according to a United Nations report provided two weeks earlier, "women and children are the main victims in the Israel-Hamas war, with some 16,000 killed and an estimated two mothers losing their lives every hour since Hamas' surprise attack on Israel." The report goes on, stating that "at least 3,000 women may have become widows and heads of households and at least 10,000 children may have lost their fathers."[4]

That same report speaks of the displacement occurring; "of the territory's 2.3 million population, it said, 1.9 million are

---

1. Richardson, "Apocalyptic Evangelism."
2. Al-Sawalhi et al., "Dozens Killed," para. 7.
3. Farge et al, "Gaza Death Toll," paras. 1 and 29.
4. Lederer, "Women and Children," paras. 1–2.

displaced and 'close to one million are women and girls' [are] seeking shelter and safety."[5]

What can we conclude about Richardson's perspective?

That because of a history of oppression and biblical prophecy, Israel's responses to Hamas's attacks were justified—including killing, injuring, and uprooting Palestinians in ways well beyond the impact of October 7? That promoting the sanctity of life is situational—to be avoided when Israel is harmed?

Standing with Israel—an absolute requirement according to him—is demanded not only because they are God's special people according to Richardson, but because they do not know Jesus: "Our job as ambassadors of Jesus, as ambassadors of the God of Israel is to call Israel back to faithfulness to their God, back to the words of Moses, and their King Yeshua [Jesus]."[6]

Being pro-life in the middle of war is difficult if not impossible. Defending your country, your land, your people is certainly morally sound. I appreciate the statement on war from the Christian Reformed Church:

> All wars are the result of sin, and although God may use war in his judgment on nations, it is his purpose to make all wars to cease. Christians are called to do all in their power to promote peace and understanding between nations and the resolution of differences without recourse to war, but they must also at times perform the solemn duty of defending their nations against aggressors. A just war is one in which the object is not to destroy or annihilate but to deter the lawless and overpower the enemy state in order to assign it to its rightful place in the family of nations. Its goal is to establish a lasting peace on the foundation of justice and a stable and righteous political order, in which human society can flourish.[7]

In the Middle East, we have been witnessing a legitimate defense going overboard, leading to a near annihilation of another

---

5. Lederer, "Women and Children," para. 3.
6. Richardson, "Apocalyptic Evangelism."
7. Christian Reformed Church in North America, "War," para 1.

people, their homes, universities, hospitals, and food sources. Stated differently, in the war against Hamas, how much collateral damage (i.e., ordinary Palestinians living in Gaza—their homes, universities, etc.) is required, tolerable? At this point in time, there seems to be little respect of ordinary human life in Israel's response. Going well beyond Hamas, their response is resulting in what some have labeled a genocide, killing ordinary Palestinian people by the thousands—and two-thirds of them women and children. So, I firmly reject Richardson's reasoning, whether leaning on Israel's status as God's special people or on the desire to save their country in order to save their souls.

There's very little new in Richardson's perspective. Known as Christian Zionists, Richardson and thousands of other evangelical Christians "have actively lobbied for both the return of Jews to modern-day Israel and for an end to the existence of the territories administered by the Palestinian Authority."[8] The theology that undergirds such thinking is "that the return of Christ will be heralded by the 'rapture'—in which true believers will be taken to meet Jesus in an otherworldly realm. However, for the majority, the rapture will be preceded by the return of Jews to the Holy Land, and the conversion of Jews to Christian belief."[9] And it is all based on the covenant God made with Abraham found in Gen 12, 15, and 17—that God promised land to Abraham, that his offspring would form a great nation, and that through his descendants, the whole earth would be blessed.

The biblical problem with such positions is the failure to include New Testament fulfillment. While all of the chosen people/nation pronouncements of the Old Testament provided an ever-present reality for the people of Israel in that era, the fulfillment in the New Testament is seen in the coming of Christ—whereby the whole world would be blessed. In Gal 3:23-29, Paul says this:

> Before the coming of this faith, we were held in custody under the law, locked up until the faith that was to come would be revealed. So the law was our guardian until

---

8. Inform, "Factsheet: Christian Zionism," para. 17.

9. Inform, "Factsheet: Christian Zionism," para. 9.

> Christ came that we might be justified by faith. Now that this faith has come, we are no longer under a guardian. So in Christ Jesus you are all children of God through faith, for all of you who were baptized into Christ have clothed yourselves with Christ. There is neither Jew nor Gentile, neither slave nor free, nor is there male and female, for you are all one in Christ Jesus. If you belong to Christ, then you are Abraham's seed, and heirs according to the promise.

It's no longer a promise to only a specific people and nation. No longer is it important to be a Jew—or a Gentile. And most importantly, through belief in Christ, we become Abraham's seed—part of his descendants by which the whole world would be blessed. No longer is the focus on a specific ethnic group or a specific land area.

If you are to be pro-life, you must be more than pro-Israeli. The war begun by Hamas in late 2023 is only a terribly unfortunate example of the issue, but it illustrates how Christian Zionism, based on incorrect theology, can support genocide-like actions of Israel at any time in recent history.

To be fully pro-life, we have to not only understand the full biblical perspective but also understand political history by going back to early in the previous century. In 1922, the League of Nations (the precursor of the United Nations) placed all of the former Ottoman territories under the authority of the United Kingdom—called the British Mandate. All became independent countries except Palestine, due in large part to colliding world events that led up to World War II: the specific area of modern-day Israel grew rapidly in the 1930s with many Eastern European Jews immigrating there due to Hitler—and that migration was accompanied by Arab resistance. Finally, the United Kingdom turned the problem over to the United Nations in 1947, who then proposed ending the British Mandate and "partitioning Palestine into two independent States, one Palestinian Arab and the other Jewish, with Jerusalem internationalized (Resolution 181 (II) of 1947)."[10]

10. United Nations, "Question of Palestine."

Notice, the United Nations called for two new countries: a Palestinian Arab country and a Jewish country. In less than a year, Israel proclaimed its statehood in 1948. As a result, over half of the Palestinian population in the new nation of Israel fled or were expelled from their homes and land. Conflict in the region continued, and a war in 1967 saw another half million Palestinians flee as Israel took over control of the Gaza Strip and the West Bank. In other words, while Israel became a country, Palestine—despite the United Nations' proposal—not only failed to become a country, but the areas to which many Palestinians fled (the Gaza Strip and the West Bank) became overseen by Israel.

Justice—truly a biblical concept that has evaded the Middle East and, in particular, the Palestinian people. Yes, we do hear calls for a "two state solution," meaning peace needs to be achieved with both Israel and Palestine as independent countries, each with their own land. Yet in the United States, the pro-Israel lobby is strong, and the idea of a two-state solution never gains traction.

Instead, recurring events continue. From the ranks of Palestinian people, terrorist groups have arisen to retaliate against the oppression and/or aggression from Israel. Hamas and Hezbollah are two recent examples. In no way is terrorism justified, but to be fully pro-life, we must also name the seventy-five plus years of the oppression of the Palestinian people. Moreover, people of Old Testament faith (i.e., the modern nation of Israel) must be held accountable for their failures and join the world in seeking a solution where all people have dignity and a right to flourish in the places they call home.

The situation in 2023–24 is bound to be repeated if we embrace Christian Zionism and ignore political history. Instead, we should listen to faith leaders closest to the situation as provided in 2006 by the Patriarch of the Catholic Church in Jerusalem, the Syrian Orthodox Archbishop in Jerusalem, the Bishop of the Episcopal Church of Jerusalem and the Middle East, and the Evangelical Lutheran Bishop in Jordan and the Holy Land:

We categorically reject Christian Zionist doctrines as false teaching that corrupts the biblical message of love, justice and reconciliation.

We further reject the contemporary alliance of Christian Zionist leaders and organizations with elements in the governments of Israel and the United States that are presently imposing their unilateral pre-emptive borders and domination over Palestine. This inevitably leads to unending cycles of violence that undermine the security of all peoples of the Middle East and the rest of the world.

We reject the teachings of Christian Zionism that facilitate and support these policies as they advance racial exclusivity and perpetual war rather than the gospel of universal love, redemption and reconciliation taught by Jesus Christ. Rather than condemn the world to the doom of Armageddon we call upon everyone to liberate themselves from the ideologies of militarism and occupation. Instead, let them pursue the healing of the nations!

We call upon Christians in Churches on every continent to pray for the Palestinian and Israeli people, both of whom are suffering as victims of occupation and militarism. These discriminative actions are turning Palestine into impoverished ghettos surrounded by exclusive Israeli settlements. The establishment of the illegal settlements and the construction of the Separation Wall on confiscated Palestinian land undermines the viability of a Palestinian state as well as peace and security in the entire region.

We call upon all Churches that remain silent, to break their silence and speak for reconciliation with justice in the Holy Land.

Therefore, we commit ourselves to the following principles as an alternative way:

We affirm that all people are created in the image of God. In turn they are called to honor the dignity of every human being and to respect their inalienable rights.

We affirm that Israelis and Palestinians are capable of living together within peace, justice and security.

We affirm that Palestinians are one people, both Muslim and Christian. We reject all attempts to subvert and fragment their unity.

We call upon all people to reject the narrow world view of Christian Zionism and other ideologies that privilege one people at the expense of others.

We are committed to non-violent resistance as the most effective means to end the illegal occupation in order to attain a just and lasting peace.

With urgency we warn that Christian Zionism and its alliances are justifying colonization, apartheid and empire-building.

God demands that justice be done. No enduring peace, security or reconciliation is possible without the foundation of justice. The demands of justice will not disappear. The struggle for justice must be pursued diligently and persistently but non-violently.

"What does the Lord require of you, to act justly, to love mercy, and to walk humbly with your God." (Micah 6:8)

This is where we take our stand. We stand for justice. We can do no other. Justice alone guarantees a peace that will lead to reconciliation with a life of security and prosperity for all the peoples of our Land. By standing on the side of justice, we open ourselves to the work of peace —and working for peace makes us children of God.

"God was reconciling the world to himself in Christ, not counting men's sins against them. And he has committed to us the message of reconciliation." (2 Cor 5:19)[11]

I believe this declaration to be a preeminent pro-life statement concerning Christians' attitudes and actions regarding the Middle East. While 99 percent of us are not engaged in diplomacy, are not called upon to lead peace talks, and are not personally engaged in the Middle East conflict, this statement calls us to reject Christian Zionism in our churches and to work for justice in our conversations and when we enter the voting booth. And as we are now honored to be part of Abraham's seed, let us be responsible believers, seeking justice and peace for all of God's children.

Thus, other areas of conflict require our attention. Russia's invasion of Ukraine is one such place. Turning back a few pages,

---

11. Sabbah et al., "Jerusalem Declaration on Christian Zionism."

recall this statement from the Christian Reformed Church's just war position: "A just war is one in which the object is not to destroy or annihilate but to deter the lawless and overpower the enemy state in order to assign it to its rightful place in the family of nations." Truly, aiding Ukraine in the war that began in February of 2022 seems to be a pro-life responsibility. Ukraine needs to be returned to and assured of its rightful place in the family of nations.

As I pen these words, there are two other disastrous and discouraging internal conflicts: in Sudan and in Haiti. The civil war in Sudan, begun in April of 2023, is due to two different military factions seeking control and power. While it may be tempting to ignore the sanctity of life when a conflict is internal, consider what a United Nations spokesperson has said:

> By all measures—the sheer scale of humanitarian needs, the numbers of people displaced and facing hunger—Sudan is one of the worst humanitarian disasters in recent memory. A humanitarian travesty is playing out in Sudan under a veil of international inattention and inaction.[12]

Much closer to the United States are the struggles in Haiti. Never with a strong government, Haiti is beset with gangs and violence. Consider this report describing the state of affairs:

> For three weeks, Haiti's capital has been trapped in a gory cycle that far exceeds the kidnapping and gang violence for which it was already known. An insurgent league of heavily armed gangs is waging war on the city itself, seeking new territory and targeting police and state institutions. Scared and angry, vigilante groups are blocking off their neighborhoods with felled trees and chains, killing and burning outsiders suspected of gang membership. It's the only way, they say, to defend themselves. Human remains are lying in the streets, yet the multinational security mission long touted by Haiti's neighbors as a game-changer for its gang problem is nowhere to be found.[13]

---

12. Al Jazeera, "Sudan 'One of the Worst,'" paras. 3–4.
13. Hu et al., "Carnage on the Streets," paras. 5–6.

The Struggle for Life in War Zones

One wonders why nations haven't delivered on the promise of a multinational security mission. Is it because the problems are so complex that reestablishment of the rule of law seems impossible? Or is there little interest in this poor, struggling nation and her people?

Whether it's Gaza, Sudan, Haiti, or conflicts yet to emerge, the challenge is to flip the paradigm from focusing on national security to the security of persons. After immense failure to ensure the security of people in Rwanda and other places around the globe, in 2005 world leaders pledged to consider their responsibilities in new ways:

> At the 2005 World Summit, all Heads of State and Government affirmed the responsibility to protect populations from genocide, war crimes, ethnic cleansing and crimes against humanity. The responsibility to protect (commonly referred to as "RtoP") rests upon three pillars of equal standing: the responsibility of each State to protect its populations (pillar I); the responsibility of the international community to assist States in protecting their populations (pillar II); and the responsibility of the international community to protect when a State is manifestly failing to protect its populations (pillar III).[14]

Clearly, this is a case of general revelation—a shared belief that people are worthy of life—acted upon by leaders of many faiths and no faith at all. Moreover, at least one denomination, the Christian Reformed Church, responded to these three pillars, explaining its congruence with belief:

> These core concepts seem consistent with many Reformed teachings, such as God as the only sovereign authority; respect for the dignity, rights, and mutual responsibilities of all persons as image-bearers of God; recognition of the power of sin and evil to distort created good; recognition of the essential but limited role of governance; and acceptance of responsibility to use power for good balanced with need for checks to prevent

---

14. Simonovic, "Responsibility to Protect," para. 1.

misuse of power and exercise mutual accountability at all levels.[15]

But before we congratulate brothers and sisters around the world on this achievement, we need to ask if it is working. The answer is barely. Pillar II demands that the international community acts when a population needs protection, and South Africa did just that when they brought charges against Israel to the International Court of Justice in December 2023:

> South Africa today filed an application instituting proceedings against Israel before the International Court of Justice (ICJ), the principal judicial organ of the United Nations, concerning alleged violations by Israel of its obligations under the Convention on the Prevention and Punishment of the Crime of Genocide (the "Genocide Convention") in relation to Palestinians in the Gaza Strip.[16]

Of course, the wheels of justice move slowly, and Israel is expert at ignoring international pressure of any kind. But it is significant that we see South Africa—a country whose majority people once needed international protection—acting out of conviction without using the tools of war.

But overall, the responsibility to protect platform is being ignored. The second pillar should provide more than sufficient rationale for countries to step forward in Gaza. And while the countries of NATO (including the United States) have responded with incredible military funding and assistance in Ukraine, recent history shows that the Republican party in Congress (the party to which much of evangelical Christianity has allied itself) has stepped back from continuing to provide much needed help. The third pillar, if taken seriously, would spur responses to the situations in Sudan and Haiti; but seemingly the international community has ignored

---

15. Christian Reformed Church in North America, "Committee to Study," 451.

16. International Court of Justice, "Republic of South Africa Institutes," para. 1.

the situation in Sudan, and the only international response to Haiti has been from just one country—Kenya—a response to send one thousand police officers that, at this writing, was still up in the air.[17]

We profess the value of life but are seemingly only paralyzed bystanders to assaults on life in so many places around the world.

Assistance in nation building should be a key purpose of our foreign policy. While this is simple to state, it is truly difficult to pursue. In our current cases of Sudan and Haiti, the weakness of their governments give rise to the conflict, but addressing those weaknesses can be a challenge, particularly when our help is not welcomed. Nevertheless, it is clear what not to do if you seek to promote life: In Donald Trump's initial term as president, he sought to put America first, and did so in an isolationist way: "A skeptic of international institutions, he has withdrawn from UN bodies governing health and human rights, major multinational agreements on climate, arms control, and Iran."[18] Truly, this is not the way to be fully for life for God's children around the globe. We can and should do better.

WHAT YOU CAN DO TO PROMOTE LIFE

In our conversations, in our social media posts, and in our giving, humanitarian aid needs to be our priority. While we may look to government for such aid, we must join hands with faith-based groups such as World Renew, World Relief, and so many others. For in current and future conflicts, people are displaced—often losing nearly everything they have. Next comes hunger and poor health for displaced people. Providing the cup of cold water in Matt 10:42 is a biblical injunction that goes well beyond hospitality, and it is our responsibility to respond with mercy. Many times, unfortunately, it's the best we can do.

---

17. Ruvaga, "Kenya Promised Cops to Haiti," para. 5.
18. Council on Foreign Relations, "Donald J. Trump," para. 1.

11

Promoting Life in a Post-Christian Era

WE'VE COMPLETED THE TOUR, and hopefully your view of what it means to be pro-life has expanded. Whether by specific revelation or general revelation, I trust you feel God's leading to cherish and promote life in multiple ways, for all of us are the crown of God's creation—we who bear God's image.

At times, you may have felt the urging to respond locally in new ways in order to love your neighbor. At other times, you may have become aware of the need to change the systems and structures of society.

Regardless of how you've reacted, my belief is that an expanded pro-life agenda must begin in the church. I can anticipate your reactions. "The situation is dire and we live in a post-Christian society. We must take action!" True, but Jesus said his kingdom was not of this world; our goal should not be to infuse Christianity into either law or government policy. We must come to terms with living in a post-Christian world and understand anew how to be salt and light, a task that begins in church—church that is neither a political action committee nor a social service agency.

It is in church that we hear the messages of Scripture, for God has revealed his great love for us and instructed us to love our neighbor as ourselves. Certainly, add to your daily ways of reaching out to your neighbor and don't enter the voting booth with only one pro-life issue in mind. But, if we are to become steeped in upholding the sanctity of life in a multitude of ways, we need to be formed—even re-formed—to become better attuned to the many threats to human life.

You may think my call to the church is focused on the pulpit. Indeed, the word of God needs to be proclaimed. Three comments on what this calls for and what it does not.

God's word begins with Creation. God created all things, and the crown of creation is humankind—we who are made in God's image. That's the point: Life is precious, a gift from God. We must not take it lightly, as I hope the preceding chapters have shown. Truly, "me and Jesus" is all important, but if we don't begin with creation, we're shortchanging the Bible and its relevance to our lives and all of the many contexts in which we live.

God's word ends with Revelation—the new kingdom and new earth. This is the vision that should drive us, by the power of the Spirit, to spend our lives in service. Streets made of gold? Yes, the infrastructures of our cities and town must be of such a quality that life is sustainable, keeping the most vulnerable from cholera, lead poisoning, and other health concerns. A gathering of those from every nation, tribe, people and language? Yes, all people come together before the Lord, so every life must be valued, whether the affluent or impoverished. When we insist that our lives (our rights, our possessions, etc.) are more important than the lives of others, we are failing to live in the light of God's restoring work among us. In short, our work must be joining in the work of restoration—restoring God's original creation toward the vision of the new kingdom and new earth.

God's word is living. It is not just stories of long ago and far away. It speaks to our present reality. Of course, at times it's challenging to understand the application to today's context. Sometimes those who promote the infallibility of Scripture use that as an excuse not to do the hard work of using an appropriate hermeneutic. I think of the church's struggle with homosexuality, and I believe the struggle to understand Scripture in today's context is difficult—but the struggle is the only way to be faithful.

Karl Barth is quoted as saying, "We must hold the Bible in one hand and the newspaper in the other." In other words, from the pulpit we must not only hear God's word, we must also discover the connection to the world in which we live. Sometimes we hear this in the sermon wrap-up; other times it dawns on us a few days later. But in either case, God's word speaks—to each of us. To stretch the metaphor (because so many young people no longer have the experience of reading a newspaper), a newspaper used to have local news, international news, financial news, governmental news, and so many other focal points. So when Barth made the statement, he meant that God's word is connected to all of our arenas of life. Singular focus is not appropriate; God's word enters into every area of our lives as well as the lives of others as we live between creation and revelation.

My interest in the church, however, is not only because of the preached word. It also must become a place of Christian learning and service. Most churches include Sunday School as a way to teach the lessons of Scripture to children. Less frequently, church includes some form of adult education to teach the application of Scripture to adults. Sometimes, particularly in the teen years, churches emphasize service with students, most often in the form of mission trips. Fewer are the churches that have figured out the analogy for adults. Yet the opportunities are many: refugee resettlement, food banks, and more.

Of course, to have the church be the center of your journey of sanctification, you have to attend. Twice a month (with soccer games in between) isn't sufficient. Sitting as a spectator in an amazing mega-church service isn't enough if it's not tied to engagement with the ministries of the church. Church attendance and involvement is the most important thing you can do, not just for your eternal destiny, but also for your short time on earth as you seek to value what God values, care for what God cares for, and love what God loves. You see, to be focused on the promotion of life in its many forms will bring flourishing to your life in faithful response to what God has done. For if we are to keep God's word in a post-Christian society, we must be anchored to God's church.

In closing, let me suggest a few easy steps.

If your advocacy has been anti-abortion, add another area of pro-life activity to your advocacy: gun violence, poverty, or any of the foci you've encountered in this book. If your church hasn't considered this new focus for you, bring it to your church and enlist others to join you.

If you've never met a refugee, an ex-offender, or a person mired in poverty, it's time. It may be awkward or artificial, but you need to begin somewhere. I'm hoping your church will show you the doorway, either via the ministries of the church or a partner organization. Learn to love a neighbor.

If you long to change laws and improve policies, you might run for office. Short of that, join a local advocacy group. It may be faith-based or part of a bigger tent. But you will soon find out the pressing needs for the flourishing of life for all in your community. Lend your voice to the discussion and show up at city hall.

Finally, if you need more time, go to church—a church that takes God's commands seriously. And read. Read God's word. Read, too, what others have written. Whether by God's specific revelation or general revelation, understand more fully what God requires of us.

And remember always the instructions from 1 John 4:7a, 11, and 21: "Dear friends, let us love one another, for love comes from God." "Dear friends, since God so loved us, we also ought to love one another." "And he has given us this command: Anyone who loves God must also love their brother and sister."

Bibliography

Abad-Santos, Alexander. "Paul Rand Isn't 100% Pro-Life Anymore." *Atlantic*, Mar. 20, 2013. www.theatlantic.com/politics/archive/2013/03/rand-paul-isnt-100-pro-life-any-more/317037/.

Al Jazeera. "Sudan One of the 'Worst Humanitarian Disasters in Recent Memory,' UN Warns." Al Jazeera, Mar. 20, 2024. https://www.aljazeera.com/news/2024/3/20/sudan-is-one-of-the-worst-humanitarian-disasters-in-recent-memory-un.

Alper, Becka A. "Religious Groups' Views on Climate Change." Pew Research Center, Nov. 17, 2022. https://www.pewresearch.org/religion/2022/11/17/religious-groups-views-on-climate-change/.

Al-Sawalhi, Mohammad, et al. "Dozens Killed During 2 Days of Airstrikes in Central and Southern Gaza, Local Medical Sources Say." CNN, Feb. 4, 2024. https://www.cnn.com/middleeast/live-news/israel-hamas-war-gaza-news-02-04-24/index.html.

Anderson, Bryan. "Critical Race Theory Is a Flashpoint for Conservatives, but What Does It Mean?" *PBS News Hour*, Nov. 4, 2021. https://www.pbs.org/newshour/education/so-much-buzz-but-what-is-critical-race-theory.

Annie E. Casey Foundation. "Child Welfare and Foster Care Statistics." May 20, 2023. https://www.aecf.org/blog/child-welfare-and-foster-care-statistics.

Balmer, Randall. "The Evangelical Abortion Myth: An Excerpt from 'Bad Faith.'" *Religion Dispatches*, Aug. 30, 2021. https://religiondispatches.org/the-evangelical-abortion-myth-an-excerpt-from-bad-faith/.

Barnes, Kate. "Properly Implemented Firearm Access Policies Are Effective at Reducing Injury, Study Finds." *Michigan News*, Aug. 14, 2023. https://news.umich.edu/properly-implemented-firearm-access-policies-are-effective-at-reducing-injury-study-finds/.

Becker, Deborah. "This Family Didn't Wait for 'Rock Bottom' to Help a Loved One with Their Addiction." *All Things Considered*, Jan. 2, 2024. https://www.npr.org/2024/01/02/1222552137/this-family-didnt-wait-for-rock-bottom-to-help-a-loved-one-with-their-addiction.

Bibliography

Belson, Ken, et al. "A Burst of Gunfire, a Pause, Then Carnage in Las Vegas That Would Not Stop." *New York Times*, Oct. 2, 2017. https://www.nytimes.com/2017/10/02/us/las-vegas-shooting-live-updates.html.

Bishop, Steve. "Everything Matters: Gordon Spykman—A Neo-Calvinist Theologian." *Pro Rege* 52.3 (Mar. 2024) 1–15.

Burger, Warren. "Second Amendment Has Been Distorted." *Record Searchlight*, Dec. 11, 1991. https://www.newspapers.com/article/102574603/record-searchlight/.

Buursma, Madalyn. "GR Makes 'Significant' Changes to Housing Rules: Here's What They Mean." *WOODTV*, Apr. 24, 2024. https://www.woodtv.com/news/grand-rapids/gr-makes-significant-changes-to-housing-rules-heres-what-they-mean/.

Campbell, Ardina. "What Is Black Lives Matter and What Are the Aims?" BBC, June 12, 2021. https://www.bbc.com/news/explainers-53337780.

Chaiken, Sarina R., et al. "Association between Rates of Down Syndrome Diagnosis in States with vs. without 20-Week Abortion Bans from 2011 to 2018." *JAMA Network Open* 6.3 (Mar. 21, 2023). https://www.ncbi.nlm.nih.gov/pmc/articles/PMC10031387/.

Chandler, Kim. "Warnings of the Impact of Fertility Treatments in Alabama Rush in after Frozen Embryo Ruling." Associated Press, Feb. 21, 2024. https://apnews.com/article/alabama-supreme-court-from-embryos-161390f0758b04a7638e2ddea20df7ca.

Chasan, Aliza. "What Are Red Flag Laws and Do They Work in Preventing Gun Violence?" CBS News, June 30, 2023. https://www.cbsnews.com/news/what-are-red-flag-laws-do-they-work-prevent-gun-violence/.

Christianity Today. "A Protestant Affirmation on the Control of Human Reproduction." Nov. 8, 1968. https://www.christianitytoday.com/ct/1968/november-8/protestant-affirmation-on-control-of-human-reproduction.html.

Cockes, Timothy. "Litton Joins California Baptists in Migrant Ministry on the Border." *Baptist Press*, Aug. 19, 2021. https://www.baptistpress.com/resource-library/news/litton-joins-california-baptists-in-migrant-ministry-on-border/.

Coghill, Arianna, and Garrison Hayes. "Elon Musk Keeps Spreading a Very Specific Kind of Racism." *Mother Jones*, Mar. 13, 2024. https://www.motherjones.com/politics/2024/03/elon-musk-racist-tweets-science-video/.

Council on Foreign Relations. "Donald J. Trump." undated. https://www.cfr.org/election2020/candidate-tracker/donald-j.-trump.

Christian Reformed Church in North America. "The Committee to Study War and Peace." Agenda for Synod 2006. https://www.crcna.org/sites/default/files/2006_agenda.pdf.

———. "War." Position Statements. https://www.crcna.org/welcome/beliefs/position-statements/war.

Bibliography

Dalen, James, et al. "Why Do So Many Americans Oppose the Affordable Care Act?" *American Journal of Medicine* 128.8 (Aug. 2015) 807–10. https://www.amjmed.com/article/S0002-9343(15)00164-3/pdf.

Degman, Alex. "Illinois Has Banned Assault Weapons, but Many Residents Aren't Complying." National Public Radio, Jan. 15, 2024. https://www.npr.org/2024/01/15/1224815782/illinois-has-banned-assault-weapons-but-many-residents-arent-complying.

Deliso, Meredith, et al. "Suspect Fired 50 Rounds in Buffalo Supermarket Hate Crime Shooting That Killed 10: Police." ABC News, May 15, 2022. https://abcnews.go.com/US/reported-mass-shooting-upstate-york-tops-supermarket/story?id=84721175.

Demby, Gene. "The Truth behind the Lies of the Original 'Welfare Queen.'" *All Things Considered*, Dec. 20, 2013. https://www.npr.org/sections/codeswitch/2013/12/20/255819681/the-truth-behind-the-lies-of-the-original-welfare-queen.

Desmond, Matthew. *Poverty, By America.* New York: Crown, 2023.

Earll, Carrie Gordon. "Abortion and Obamacare." Focus on the Family, Jan. 1, 2014. https://www.focusonthefamily.com/pro-life/abortion-and-obamacare/.

Elving, Ron. "The U.S. Once Had a Ban on Assault Weapons—Why Did It Expire?" National Public Radio, Aug. 13, 2019. https://www.npr.org/2019/08/13/750656174/the-u-s-once-had-a-ban-on-assault-weapons-why-did-it-expire.

De Bres, Guido. *The Belgic Confession.* 1561. https://www.crcna.org/welcome/beliefs/confessions/belgic-confession.

Dreier, Peter. "Reagan's Legacy: Homelessness in America." Shelterforce: Essential Reporting on Affordable Housing, May 1, 2004. https://shelterforce.org/2004/05/01/reagans-legacy-homelessness-in-america/.

Erickson, Blake. "Deinstitutionalization through Optimism: The Community Health Act of 1963." *American Journal of Psychiatry* 16.4 (June 11, 2021) 6–7. https://ajp.psychiatryonline.org/doi/10.1176/appi.ajp-rj.2021.160404.

Farge, Emma, et al. "Gaza Death Toll: How Many Palestinians Has Israel's Campaign Killed." Reuters, July 10, 2024. https://www.reuters.com/world/middle-east/gaza-death-toll-how-many-palestinians-has-israels-campaign-killed-2024-05-14/.

Gamboa, Suzanne. "No Allies Left: Dreamers, DACA Recipients Are Left Out amid Rightward Shift on Immigration." NBC News, Feb. 10, 2024. https://www.nbcnews.com/news/latino/congress-ignores-dreamers-daca-recipients-immigration-rcna137725.

Gilligan, Chris. "U.S. Remains an Outlier in Firearm Possession, Gun-Related Deaths." *U.S. News and World Report*, January 30, 2023. https://www.usnews.com/news/best-countries/articles/2023-01-30/how-the-u-s-compares-to-the-world-on-guns.

Bibliography

Gold, Rachel Benson. "The Implications of Defining When a Woman Is Pregnant." The Guttmacher Institute, May 9, 2005. https://www.guttmacher.org/gpr/2005/05/implications-defining-when-woman-pregnant.

Goldstein, Emily, and Mandi Cai. "What Do Migrants Experience When They Request Asylum at the Texas-Mexico Border?" *Texas Tribune*, July 22, 2019. https://www.texastribune.org/2019/07/22/asylum-seekers-experience-texas-mexico-border/.

Gotlib, I. H., et al. "Effects of the COVID-19 Pandemic on Mental Health and Brain Maturation in Adolescents: Implications for Analyzing Longitudinal Data." *Biological Psychiatry Global Open Science* 3.4 (Jan. 26, 2023) 912–18. https://doi.org/10.1016/j.bpsgos.2022.11.002.

Grcevich, Stephen. "What Are the Stats on Adoption, Trauma and Disability." Church4EveryChild, Feb. 16, 2016. https://church4everychild.org/2016/02/16/what-are-the-stats-on-adoption-trauma-and-disability/.

Gross, Terry. "A 'Forgotten History' of How the U.S. Government Segregated America." *Fresh Air*, May 3, 2017. https://www.npr.org/2017/05/03/526655831/a-forgotten-history-of-how-the-u-s-government-segregated-america.

Guevara, Selina, and Erik Ortiz. "James Crumbley, Father of Ethan Crumbley, Found Guilty of Involuntary Manslaughter in Son's School Shooting." NBC News, Mar. 14, 2024. https://www.nbcnews.com/news/us-news/verdict-james-crumbley-involuntary-manslaughter-trial-rcna143174.

Hardy, Bradley, et al. "The Antipoverty Effects of the Expanded Child Tax Credit across States: Where Were the Historic Reductions Felt?" Brookings Institution, March 2023. https://www.brookings.edu/articles/the-antipoverty-effects-of-the-expanded-child-tax-credit-across-states-where-were-the-historic-reductions-felt/.

Holst, Jan. "College Student Starts School for Kids in Ethiopia." *The Cadence/MLive*, Jan. 15, 2017.

Horton, Robert S. "From Convict to Mentor: Changing the Prison Culture from Within." *Reformed Journal*, Apr. 8, 2024. reformedjournal.com/from-convict-to-mentor-changing-the-prison-culture-from-within/?fbclid=IwAR2zDYOxOpZrRoz1uB-U7futPfAVkK4OcRriiRG4hMohCgDnzjyz4x26I8g_aem_AdJ1jr1lK614fZO-pzDNtfbupdbqbPEP46DSPi_PX_pMJ3XmBOU7sk7ouMRkRFCELVsTydkK11FbrcGgRpvFYPr7.

Howard, Ron, dir. *A Beautiful Mind*. Universal City, CA: Universal Pictures/Dreamworks, 2001. DVD.

Hu, Caitlin Stephen, et al. "Carnage on the Streets in Port-au-Prince as World Stalls on a Promised Intervention for Haiti." CNN, Mar. 22, 2024. www.cnn.com/2024/03/21/americas/haiti-council-gang-intl-latam/index.html.

Indiana University Health. "Is Addiction Really a Disease?" *Thrive by IU Health*, Sept. 2, 2020. https://iuhealth.org/thrive/is-addiction-really-a-disease.

BIBLIOGRAPHY

Inform. "Factsheet: Christian Zionism." Religion Media Centre, Feb. 21, 2022. https://religionmediacentre.org.uk/factsheets/factsheet-christian-zionism/.

International Court of Justice. "The Republic of South Africa Institutes Proceedings against the State of Israel." Press release no. 2023/77, Dec. 29, 2023. https://www.icj-cij.org/sites/default/files/case-related/192/192-20231229-pre-01-00-en.pdf.

Jones, Casey. "Low-Income Grocer Offers Dignity through Ownership." WOODTV, Apr. 1, 2024. http://www.woodtv.com/community/community-spotlight/low-income-grocer-offers-dignity-through-ownership/.

King, Martin Luther, Jr. *Why We Can't Wait*. New York: Harper & Row, 1964.

Kirzinger, Ashley, et al. "Five Charts about Public Opinion on the Affordable Care Act." KFF, Feb. 22, 2014. https://www.kff.org/affordable-care-act/poll-finding/5-charts-about-public-opinion-on-the-affordable-care-act/.

Klobucista, Claire, et al. "How Does the U.S. Refugee System Work?" Council on Foreign Relations, Feb. 15, 2023. https://www.cfr.org/backgrounder/how-does-us-refugee-system-work-trump-biden-afghanistan.

Kolker, Ken. "Ruby Garcia Murder Suspect Spent Night at Church before Turning Himself In." WOODTV, Apr. 4, 2024. https://www.woodtv.com/news/target-8/ruby-garcia-murder-suspect-spent-night-at-church-before-turning-himself-in/.

Korhonen, Veera. "Number of Refugee Admissions in the U.S. 1990 to 2023." Statista, Nov. 17, 2023. http://statista.com/statistics/200061/number-of-refugees-arriving-in-the-us/.

Lederer, Edith. "Women and Children Are the Main Victims of the Israel-Hamas War with 16,000 Killed, UN Says." Associated Press, Jan. 19, 2024. https://apnews.com/article/women-children-gaza-war-victims-un-inequality-f0f89a724543b99c2c22439e7af09405.

Li, Irena. "Tight Labor Market Helps Michigan's Ex-Prisoners Find Jobs." *Bridge Michigan*, July 14, 2023. https://www.bridgemi.com/business-watch/tight-labor-market-helps-michigans-ex-prisoners-find-jobs.

Lile, Jennifer. "Adopting a Child with Special Needs." Special Needs Alliance, undated. https://www.specialneedsalliance.org/blog/adopting-a-child-with-special-needs/.

Lopez, Mark Hugo, et al. "Key Facts about the Changing U.S. Unauthorized Immigrant Population." Pew Research Center, Apr. 13, 2021. https://www.pewresearch.org/short-reads/2021/04/13/key-facts-about-the-changing-u-s-unauthorized-immigrant-population/.

Luk, Jeremy W., et al. "Sexual Orientation and Depressive Symptoms in Adolescents." *Pediatrics* 141.5 (May 2018). https://www.ncbi.nlm.nih.gov/pmc/articles/PMC5931790/.

Mallenbaum, Carly. "Embryo 'Adoption': IVF Off-Shoot Gains Popularity." *Axios*, July 27, 2023. https://www.axios.com/2023/07/27/embryo-adoption-increase-what-it-is.

Bibliography

Mandavilli, Apoorva. "Reaching Herd Immunity Is Unlikely in the U.S. Experts Now Believe." *New York Times*, July 21, 2021. https://www.nytimes.com/2021/05/03/health/covid-herd-immunity-vaccine.html.

McCorvey, J. J. "Free Cash Programs Spread as More Cities Expand the Anti-Poverty Safety Net." NBC News, Apr. 13, 2024. https://www.nbcnews.com/business/economy/guaranteed-income-programs-spread-cities-expand-anti-poverty-safety-ne-rcna146645.

Miller, Paul D. "What Is Christian Nationalism?" *Christianity Today*, Feb. 3, 2021. https://www.christianitytoday.com/ct/2021/february-web-only/what-is-christian-nationalism.html.

Montgomery, David, et al. "Gunman Kills at Least 26 in Attack on Rural Texas Church." *New York Times*, Nov. 5, 2017. https://www.nytimes.com/2017/11/05/us/church-shooting-texas.html.

National Constitution Center. "On This Day, a Divided Supreme Court Rules on the Second Amendment." June 28, 2023. https://constitutioncenter.org/blog/on-this-day-a-divided-supreme-court-rules-on-the-second-amendment.

National Immigration Forum. "Fact Sheet: Immigrants and Public Benefits." August 2018. https://immigrationforum.org/wp-content/uploads/2018/08/Immigrants-and-Public-Benefits-FINALupdated.pdf.

National Institute on Alcohol Abuse and Alcoholism. "Treatment for Alcohol Problems." Alcohol's Effect on Health, 2014. https://www.niaaa.nih.gov/publications/brochures-and-fact-sheets/treatment-alcohol-problems-finding-and-getting-help.

National Rifle Association. "Gun Ownership Provides Effective Self-Defense." 1992. https://www.ojp.gov/ncjrs/virtual-library/abstracts/gun-ownership-provides-effective-self-defense-gun-control-p-142-149.

Nowakowski, Audrey, and Rob Larry. "1944 GI Bill: A Clear Example of Systemic Racism for the 1.2M Black Veterans Who Couldn't Benefit." *WUWM*, June 26, 2023. https://www.wuwm.com/2023-06-26/1944-gi-bill-a-clear-example-of-systemic-racism-for-the-1-2m-black-veterans-who-couldnt-benefit.

Oxner, Reese. "Uvalde Gunman Legally Bought AR Rifles Days before Shooting, Law Enforcement Says." *Texas Tribune*, May 25, 2022. https://www.texastribune.org/2022/05/25/uvalde-shooter-bought-gun-legally/.

Passel, Jeffrey, and Jens Manuel Krogstad. "What We Know about Unauthorized Immigrants Living in the U.S." Pew Research Center, Nov. 16, 2023. https://www.pewresearch.org/short-reads/2023/11/16/what-we-know-about-unauthorized-immigrants-living-in-the-us/.

Perkins, John. *Let Justice Roll Down*. Ventura, CA: Regal Books, 1976.

Peter G. Peterson Foundation. "The Share of Americans without Health Insurance Matched a Record Low in 2022." Nov. 9, 2023. https://www.pgpf.org/blog/2023/11/the-share-of-americans-without-health-insurance-in-2022-matched-a-record-low.

Bibliography

Pew Research Center. "America's Abortion Quandary." May 2022. https://www.pewresearch.org/religion/2022/05/06/americas-abortion-quandary/.

Richardson, Joel. "Apocalyptic Evangelism." Reslife Church, Feb. 4, 2024. https://www.reslife.org/sermon/apocalyptic-evangelism.

Rivera, Salvador. "80% of Asylum Seekers Rejected, DHS Spokesperson Says." WOODTV, Feb. 11, 2024. https://www.woodtv.com/news/national/80-of-asylum-seekers-rejected-dhs-official-says/.

Robertson, Campbell, et al. "11 Killed in Synagogue Massacre." New York Times, Oct. 27, 2018. https://www.nytimes.com/2018/10/27/us/active-shooter-pittsburgh-synagogue-shooting.html.

Rosenbaum, Sara. "The Patient Protection and Affordable Care Act: Implications for Public Health Policy and Practice." *Public Health Reports* 126.1 (Jan.–Feb. 2011) 130–35. https://www.ncbi.nlm.nih.gov/pmc/articles/PMC3001814/.

Rovner, Julie. "Repealing the Affordable Care Act? What a Second Trump Term May Mean for Health Care." *USA Today*, Jan. 26, 2024. https://www.usatoday.com/story/news/health/2024/01/23/trump-health-care-plan-second-term/72280611007/.

Ruvaga, Lenny. "Kenya Promised Cops to Haiti. Its Citizens Didn't Like That." *Christian Science Monitor*, Mar. 25, 2024. www.csmonitor.com/World/Africa/2024/0325/Kenya-promised-cops-to-Haiti.-Its-citizens-didn-t-like-that.

Sabbah, Michel, et al. "Jerusalem Declaration on Christian Zionism." Electronic Intifada, Aug. 31, 2006. https://electronicintifada.net/content/jerusalem-declaration-christian-zionism/627.

Scanzoni, Letha. *Sex Is a Parent Affair*. Glendale, CA: G/L Publications, 1973.

Schaeffer, Katherine. "Key Facts about Americans and Guns." Pew Research Center, Sept. 13, 2023. https://www.pewresearch.org/short-reads/2023/09/13/key-facts-about-americans-and-guns/.

Schnurer, Eric. "Just How Wrong Is Conventional Wisdom about Government Fraud?" *Atlantic*, Aug. 15, 2013. https://www.theatlantic.com/politics/archive/2013/08/just-how-wrong-is-conventional-wisdom-about-government-fraud/278690/.

Sider, Ron. *Completely Pro-Life: Building a Consistent Stance on Abortion, the Family, Nuclear Weapons, the Poor*. Carol Stream, IL: InterVarsity Press, 1987.

Simonovic, Ivan. "The Responsibility to Protect." *UN Chronicle* 53.4 (Dec. 2016). https://www.un.org/en/chronicle/article/responsibility-protect#:~:text=The%20responsibility%20to%20protect%20(commonly,and%20the%20responsibility%20of%20the.

Smith, Andrew. "Rutgers Researchers Delve Deep into the Genetics of Addiction." *Rutgers Today*, Nov. 2, 2022. https://www.rutgers.edu/news/rutgers-researchers-delve-deep-genetics-addiction.

BIBLIOGRAPHY

Soerens, Matthew. "The Border Is a Mess; What Can Christians Do to Help?" *Holy Post*, Nov. 20, 2023. https://www.holypost.com/post/the-border-is-a-mess-what-can-christians-do.

Spagat, Elliot. "Immigrants Waiting 10 Years in the US Just to Get a Court Date." Associated Press, Apr. 26, 2023. https://apnews.com/article/immigration-courts-wait-54bb5f7c18c4c37c6ca7f28231ffoedf.

Spencer, John. "Sojourner." *Oxford Bibliographies*, June 26, 2019. https://www.oxfordbibliographies.com/display/document/obo-9780195393361/obo-9780195393361-0266.xml.

Stob, Henry. *Ethical Reflections: Essays on Moral Themes*. Grand Rapids: Eerdmans, 1978.

Stogsdill, Shayla. "Children with Disabilities in the Foster Care System." *Pillars at Taylor University*, Spring 2019. https://pillars.taylor.edu/cgi/viewcontent.cgi?article=1003&context=ovc-student.

Sullivan, Becky. "Kyle Rittenhouse Is Acquitted of All Charges in the Trial over Killing 2 in Kenosha." National Public Radio, Nov. 19, 2021. https://www.npr.org/2021/11/19/1057288807/kyle-rittenhouse-acquitted-all-charges-verdict.

Sy, Stephanie, and Karina Cuevas. "Child Poverty Increases Sharply Following Expiration of Expanded Tax Credit." *PBS News Hour*, Sept. 22, 2023. https://www.pbs.org/newshour/show/child-poverty-increases-sharply-following-expiration-of-expanded-tax-credit.

Telford, Taylor. "Five Key Moments from Elon Musk's Interview with Don Lemon." *Washington Post*, Mar. 18, 2024. https://www.washingtonpost.com/technology/2024/03/18/elon-musk-don-lemon-interview/.

Totenberg, Nina, and Sarah McCammon. "Supreme Court Overturns Roe v. Wade, Ending Right to Abortion Upheld for Decades." National Public Radio, June 24, 2022. https://www.npr.org/2022/06/24/1102305859/supreme-court-abortion-roe-v-wade-decision-overturn.

Thurman, Howard. *Jesus and the Disinherited*. New York: Abingdon, 1976.

Travis, Jeremy, et al., eds. *The Growth of Incarceration in the United States: Exploring Causes and Consequences*. National Academies Press, 2014. https://nicic.gov/resources/nic-library/all-library-items/growth-incarceration-united-states-exploring-causes-and.

United Nations. "The Question of Palestine." undated. https://www.un.org/unispal/history/.

United States Census Bureau. "How the Census Bureau Measures Poverty." June 15, 2023. https://www.census.gov/topics/income-poverty/poverty/guidance/poverty-measures.html.

———. "National Poverty in America Awareness." Press release no. CB24-SFS.003, January 2024. https://www.census.gov/newsroom/stories/poverty-awareness-month.html.

United States Department of Education. "A History of the Individuals with Disabilities Education Act." undated. https://sites.ed.gov/idea/IDEA-History.

Bibliography

United States Department of Labor. "Americans with Disabilities Act." undated. https://www.dol.gov/general/topic/disability/ada.

United Way. "About Us: Meet ALICE." undated. https://www.unitedforalice.org/meet-alice.

Valverde, Miriam. "Jeff Sessions' False Claim That 80% of Asylum Applications Are without Merit." Politifact, July 2, 2018. https://www.politifact.com/factchecks/2018/jul/02/jeff-sessions/jeff-sesssions-false-claim-80-percent-asylum-appli/.

Wang, Leah, and Wanda Bertram. "New Data on Formerly Incarcerated People's Employment Reveal Labor Market Injustices." Prison Policy Initiative, Feb. 28, 2022. https://www.prisonpolicy.org/blog/2022/02/08/employment/.

Widra, Emily, and Tiana Herring. "States of Incarceration: The Global Context 2021." Prison Policy Initiative, September 2021. https://www.prisonpolicy.org/global/2021.html.

Wilson, Rebecca F., et al. "Unintentional Firearm Injury Deaths among Children and Adolescents Aged 0–17 years." Centers for Disease Control and Prevention, *Morbidity and Mortality Weekly Report*, Dec. 15, 2023. https://www.cdc.gov/mmwr/volumes/72/wr/mm7250a1.htm.

World Health Organization. "Coronavirus Disease (COVID-19): Herd Immunity, Lockdowns, and COVID-19." Dec. 31, 2020. https://www.who.int/news-room/questions-and-answers/item/herd-immunity-lockdowns-and-covid-19.

World Justice Project. "Democracy's Last Line of Defense: Preserving an Independent Judiciary." Mar. 19, 2024. https://worldjusticeproject.org/news/democracy%E2%80%99s-last-line-defense-preserving-independent-judiciary.

———. "What the Data Says about Criminal Justice Systems around the World." Feb. 13, 2019. https://worldjusticeproject.org/news/what-data-says-about-criminal-justice-systems-around-world.

Yancey, Philip. "Lessons from Rock Bottom." *Christianity Today*, July 11, 2000. https://www.christianitytoday.com/ct/2000/july10/33.72.html.

Zambelich, Ariel, and Alyson Hurt. "Three Hours in Orlando: Piecing Together an Attack and Its Aftermath." National Public Radio, June 26, 2016. https://www.npr.org/2016/06/16/482322488/orlando-shooting-what-happened-update.

www.ingramcontent.com/pod-product-compliance
Lightning Source LLC
Chambersburg PA
CBHW072154160426
43197CB00012B/2380